Toast of the Coast

FIRST IN THE SERIES FROM

The Junior League of Jacksonville

COOKBOOK COLLECTION

To purchase copies of *Toast of the Coast*,
visit us online at **www.juniorleagueofjax.org**
or call the Junior League of Jacksonville at 904-387-9927.

Toast of the Coast

The Junior League of Jacksonville

COOKBOOK COLLECTION

Toast of the Coast

VOLUME 1 OF THE JUNIOR LEAGUE OF JACKSONVILLE COOKBOOK COLLECTION

The Junior League of Jacksonville, Inc., is a 501(c) (3) nonprofit organization of women committed
to promoting voluntarism, developing the potential of women, and improving the community through the effective
action and leadership of trained volunteers. Its purpose is exclusively educational and charitable.

Proceeds from the sale of this cookbook will be reinvested in the community through Junior League of Jacksonville projects.

The Junior League of Jacksonville, Inc.
2165 Park Street
Jacksonville, Florida 32204
904-387-9927

© 2005 by
The Junior League of Jacksonville, Inc.

Photography ©The Junior League of Jacksonville, Inc.

ISBN: 0-9609338-2-4
Library of Congress Number: 2004110232

Edited, designed, and manufactured by
Favorite Recipes® Press

FRP™

P.O. Box 305142
Nashville, Tennessee 37230
800-358-0560

Book Design: Sheri Ferguson
Art Director: Steve Newman
Project Editor: Judy Jackson

Manufactured in the United States of America
First Printing: 2005
15,000 copies

This cookbook is a collection of favorite recipes, which are not necessarily original recipes.

We open our doors and greet our guests. The anticipated event begins; there is so much to celebrate!

Invitations are extended, special food and drink selected—now for the cooking. A special occasion can be taking time to gather with family and friends, an elaborate seasonal buffet, or anything in between. Savor each moment, from raising a glass to sharing a special dessert.

Toast of the Coast will inspire you with creative menus, delectable foods, and helpful entertaining tips. You will find easy recipes for an elegant luncheon, tailgate picnic, holiday open house, and more. Look ahead for a celebration of First Coast favorites indicative of our coastal climate and abundant sunshine.

When you bid farewell to your last guest, you will be secretly planning for that next special occasion, reaching for yet another recipe from *Toast of the Coast*—a celebration of First Coast favorites, beachfront to riverfront.

—THE *Toast of the Coast* COMMITTEE

Contents

page 10

page 14

page 18

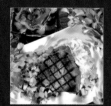

page 22

page 26

Contents

page 32

page 50

page 70

page 86

page 106

Introduction

The Junior League of Jacksonville is an organization of women committed to promoting voluntarism, developing the potential of women, and improving the community through the effective action and leadership of trained volunteers.

Formed in 1923, the Junior League of Jacksonville's early projects included a childcare center for working mothers, a well baby clinic, a clothes chest for needy families, and a milk fund for babies. The League has stayed true to its roots—today, our primary focus areas are education and at-risk children.

Our trained members spend countless hours in the community each year. This has enabled the Junior League to identify community needs and find solutions. The Junior League was instrumental in starting the Jacksonville Children's Museum (now the Museum of Science and History); the Greater Jacksonville Open (now the Players Championship); Volunteer Jacksonville; the Arts Assembly of Jacksonville; Leadership Jacksonville; CANVAS; the Bridge of Northeast Florida, Inc.; and the Family Nurturing Centers of Florida.

Focusing our efforts makes it possible to provide more impact. The Jacksonville League has long been active in the area of foster care. From collaborating with child-serving agencies to develop a nationally modeled meeting place for children and families in the foster care system to providing "bundles of love" to children entering protective custody, the League is proud to be a safe haven to the 2,800 local children entering protective custody each year.

Our passion for literacy is evident in the long-running reading program we sponsored at local elementary schools and the new initiative developed around strengthening and supporting the school, child, and family to improve literacy and all aspects of education.

Done-In-A-Day workdays continue to be the hallmark of the Junior League by providing trained volunteers to agencies and organizations for special projects that can be completed in one day. Painting murals in playrooms, organizing events, making food baskets, and sprucing up a shelter are just some of the needs filled by Junior League volunteers.

By purchasing *Toast of the Coast*, you are helping us realize our vision to be a force of change as we strive to improve the quality of life in our community.

Special thanks to our cookbook contributors for their gracious support

Contributors

SPONSORS

Belk

Fidelity National Financial

Winn-Dixie

Glenn Certain Floral Design Studio

The Grotto Wine & Tapas Bar

Gourmet Goose

PHOTOGRAPHY BY Daryl J. Bunn

FOOD STYLING BY Sherry R. Warner

COOKBOOK DEVELOPMENT COMMITTEE

Chairman
Connie Phillips

Vice-Chairman
Caroline Busker

Lynn Bailey • Kristen Chmielewski • Kelley Downey • Heather Fouts • Christy Hilpert
Suzannah Holway • Jeffrie Hood • Kami Lawson • Stacey Lewis • Bonnie McCormick
Julie McLaurine • Jean Mitchell • Nancy Pedrick • Edi Rose • Jenifer Worley

Deborah Moore, President 2003-2004

Fairway Brunch

~

MENU

Jacksonville has more than 1,000 public and private golf courses. Golf enthusiasts arrive from all over the world to swing their clubs on the immaculately manicured greens and breathe in our coastal air.

Jacksonville is also home to the headquarters of the PGA TOUR, located in Ponte Vedra Beach. The World Golf Foundation and Hall of Fame are based on the First Coast, just a bit further south in St. Augustine.

Tee time may be any time of day, so local residents favor a traditional fairway brunch. Brunch enables early birds just coming off the course an opportunity to share their success of the day and feed their ravished appetites. For golfers who like to head out in the afternoon, brunch provides energy and allows for friendly conversation before the clubs start flying.

When hosting a fairway brunch, incorporate your theme from the start. A package of scorecards from your local pro shop may make perfect invitations. Most scorecards fold in half and sometimes into thirds. Handwrite or use your computer to print on solid color paper the date, time, location, and anything

your guests need to bring. Glue the paper inside the scorecard. Fold, place in envelopes, and send them on their way.

Continue the theme by using other golf items as decorations. Golf tees, balls, and clubs are inspired additions to a table setting. If you're feeling creative, you can make your own "hole flag" toothpicks. Draw or trace a diamond shape on sticker paper, write in a hole number (1-18), cut out the diamond, and wrap around a plain toothpick so that the points meet. Instant hole flag! If you're serving food buffet style, you can even label your menu items with larger versions of these attached to golf tees.

Fairway Brunch

CHAMPAGNE AND ORANGE JUICE MIMOSAS

BLOODY BULLDAWGS WITH TIPSY TOMATOES

MINIATURE ONION QUICHES

MAYPORT SHRIMP AND GRITS

SUNRISE FRENCH TOAST

PARTY EGGS

BLUEBERRY CRUMB CAKE

ALMOND CRÈME STRAWBERRIES

RICOTTA CHEESE PIE

Mother Daughter Luncheon

~

MENU

The South is known for ladies who lunch. Rather than meet at fancy restaurants, we tend to have small, intimate parties in our homes or gardens. Whether for a bridal shower, baby shower, birthday celebration, or the first blooms of spring, luncheons are a time-honored tradition.

A fabulous way to celebrate a special occasion would be to include all generations, from the newest baby girl to her great-grandmother. For an elegant luncheon, ask everyone to wear their favorite Sunday attire. Set the table with treasured family linens, china, and silver. Include small silver vases of seasonal flowers or match flowers to your theme.

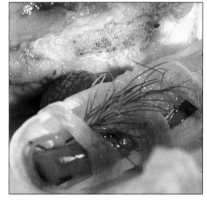

If you are hosting a bridal shower, choose colors based on those the bride has selected for her special day. For a baby shower, incorporate colors the parents have used to decorate the nursery. Primary colors are acceptable if pastels don't suit your taste. Simple bundles of white roses, daisies, alstromeria, and baby's breath can create an understated yet elegant touch for any theme.

Since a luncheon is generally a chance to have wonderful conversations with those in attendance, choose music that is soothing and relaxing. This will ensure that your guests enjoy a leisurely afternoon affair.

Outdoor conditions on the First Coast can change at the drop of a hat, so be sure to plan for inclement or unseasonable weather. In the event of rain, ask a friend or your daughter to watch for arriving guests through the window. As the guest's car comes to a stop, send her to the car with an umbrella, offering much-needed shelter and an extra set of hands. It's very difficult to juggle gifts, food, and an umbrella while trying to stay dry! If you're hosting an outdoor luncheon, tent rental is a wonderful idea. Not only does it protect your guests and the food in the event of rain, but it also provides relief from the sun.

Most of all, remember that this is a gathering of very special people. Prepare in advance and set a goal to relax and enjoy your guests.

Mother Daughter Luncheon

CAVA SANGRIA

ASPARAGUS IN ENDIVE

STUFFED CHERRY TOMATOES

RASPBERRY CHICKEN

ST. AUGUSTINE SALAD

MARINATED VEGETABLES

BRIDE'S PIE

Game Day Tailgate Picnic

~

Football is one of the South's great passions. Jacksonville plays home to some of the most famous football traditions in the country. It goes without saying that football is not just a three- to four-hour game. Football is a twenty-four hour event, which begins and ends with tailgating.

With Jacksonville's many rivers, we have the unique opportunity of tailgating by boat! You may not be as fortunate, but that doesn't mean you can't find a great shady location around the football stadium to set up for the day. If you know in advance where you'll be, send a map to your friends. You don't want anyone getting lost amid the myriad cars, SUVs, and RVs!

Before you enter football season, pack yourself a tailgate basket that can be easily loaded and unloaded from boat or car with the following items:

vinyl tablecloth for easy cleanup, plastic trash bags, utensils and cups, paper napkins and towels, wet napkins for sticky cleanups, charcoal or gas for the grill, cooking utensils, bottle opener, and fun-spirited items such as pom-poms, beads, or pennants in your team's colors.

What if your team isn't close by? No problem! Set up a tailgate in your backyard. Pitch a small tent decorated in your team's colors. Include radios or televisions so that you and your guests can catch the game while munching on great food. Use large galvanized buckets, readily available at most hardware stores, to keep your selection of lager beer ice-cold and within easy reach. Small galvanized buckets make stylish utensil holders or even a wine cooler. And remember, no southern tailgate is complete without the bourbon!

Game Day
Tailgate Picnic

BLEU CHEESE CLAM DIP

MANGO AND CORN SALSA

LONDON BROIL SANDWICHES

CHICKEN PESTO WITH BOW TIES

STRAWBERRY SPINACH SALAD

PEANUT BUTTER CHOCOLATE BARS

BOATER'S BUTTER CAKE

ASSORTED LAGER BEER

BOURBON AND COLA

Supper Club

~

MENU

Opening your home for dinner with friends, neighbors, or co-workers—or any other special group for that matter—is a wonderful way to create and strengthen personal connections while sharing great food and conversation. From pre-planned supper clubs to casual, impromptu meals, the important thing is connecting with special people.

Supper clubs can be an adults-only affair for which jackets are required, a girls-only book club gathering, a wine tasting and supper for six, or a potluck for twenty. No matter what the size or venue, make it a memorable event. Develop your theme according to the month or season of the year. Themes may celebrate distinct holidays, such as Chinese New Year in January, Cinco de Mayo in May, or Columbus Day in October. You may even adopt a local festival as your theme: Azalea, Peanut, Shrimp, or Strawberry. All make wonderful supper club themes!

Choose your food, music, serving pieces, and wine based upon the theme. For a March Madness party, invite your guests to bring a food item that is round.

For a Mardi Gras party, find authentic Cajun zydeco music and ask everyone to wear Mardi Gras beads. Whatever the theme, attendees will enjoy getting in the spirit by contributing an inspired addition to the party.

A seated dinner with friends, old or new, can be even more interesting through creative planned seating. Use themed place cards to seat guests next to someone they will enjoy talking to. Remember, guests don't always need to sit with the person they arrived with.

Another important ingredient is lighting. Candles placed throughout the house provide an intimate setting—and, as we all know, everyone looks fabulous in candlelight.

This Summer Sunset Supper Club menu includes some First Coast favorites. The tropical flavors will pair well with shades of red, yellow, orange, pink, and raspberry in your linens, flowers, and candles. Tropical or jazz music playing in the background lends nicely to the atmosphere.

Supper Club

CRAB TARTLETS

SAVORY BRUSCHETTA

TUNA WITH MANGO RELISH

WASABI MASHED POTATOES

FRESH TOMATO SALAD

MOUSSE AU CHOCOLATE IN COOKIE CUPS

SELECTION OF LIGHT WINES,

SUCH AS

A SAUVIGNON BLANC FROM NEW ZEALAND,

A DRY RIESLING FROM AUSTRALIA, OR

A PINOT GRIS FROM OREGON, OR

A PINOT GRIGIO FROM ITALY

Luminaria Open House

~

MENU

Open your home and welcome the holidays with tradition and seasonal elegance. Perfect for this busy time of year, an open house allows guests to visit your home between office parties and hectic shopping trips while sharing holiday wishes with family and friends.

The many historic neighborhoods of Jacksonville have turned this tradition into a must-attend holiday event. As the sun sets, luminaries are lit along the quaint neighborhood streets, lighting the path from house to house. Partygoers and visitors out for an evening drive arrive anytime after sunset to see the magnificent welcome that is created.

You can start this tradition in your own neighborhood by purchasing white paper bags, weighting them with sand or pebbles, and placing tea light candles on top of the filling. Use them to line the pathways and drive of your home. Get your neighbors into the spirit by delivering luminaria kits, along with dates you plan to light the night.

For your holiday-inspired open house, greet guests at the front door with a seasonal beverage; welcome them to the party and introduce them to unfamiliar faces. If you plan to invite fifty or more guests, consider hiring someone to clear empty dishes, keep food trays full, and direct guests. This may be a professional, or you can try a more cost-effective neighborhood teenager or college student. Since an open house can span a wide range of time, ensure that the foods you serve maintain their proper temperatures to keep people healthy for the holidays.

For large parties, you need to check with local officials regarding your area's rules on street parking. If possible, see if a nearby church or business will allow you to use their parking lot for party cars. If this option is available, you might want to hire a valet service or have a friend or family member direct attendees as they arrive.

As far as decorations are concerned, use whatever you already put up for the holidays! Lots of candlelight and festive music will add the finishing touches to your event.

Luminaria Open House

SPICED CRANBERRY TEA PUNCH

ASIAGO PUFFS

ROASTED RED POTATO BITES

CHICKEN PESTO TARTS

SHRIMP BUTTER

STRAWBERRY PRESERVES

BAKED BRIE EN CROÛTE

PEPPERCORN PORK TENDERLOIN

FUDGE TRUFFLE CHEESECAKE

MINIATURE PECAN PIES

RUM CONFECTIONS

MOLASSES CRINKLES

Using this guideline will help you be stress-free when the doorbell rings.

FOUR TO SIX WEEKS AHEAD

▼ Decide on a date and time.
▼ Create a guest list.
▼ Choose a theme.
▼ Select or make invitations.
▼ Order any food to be catered.

THREE TO FOUR WEEKS AHEAD

▼ Mail invitations (for informal events, mail two weeks ahead).
▼ Check your supply of chairs, linens, plates, serving ware, and silverware.
▼ Make party favors if doing so.

TWO WEEKS AHEAD

▼ Make a shopping list (include food, alcoholic beverages, flowers, and decorations).
▼ Shop for non-perishables.
▼ Plant seasonal flowers to freshen up the exterior of your home, especially if your event is being held outside.

TWO TO THREE DAYS AHEAD

▼ Shop for perishables.
▼ Make any food items that can be prepared ahead.
▼ Clean the house.
▼ Make place cards.

ONE DAY AHEAD

▼ Chill beverages and make extra ice.
▼ Decorate your home.
▼ Set the table.

DAY OF THE EVENT

▼ Prepare your centerpiece.
▼ Finish preparing your food and arrange it on serving platters. Make backup trays for replenishing during the event.
▼ Relax, smile, and enjoy.

Getting Started

If you are planning to have an open bar for the evening, you will want to make certain it is well stocked.

SOME GUIDELINES FOR A FULL BAR ARE AS FOLLOWS:

Mixers	Cola, lemon-lime soda, tonic water, club soda, seltzer, ginger ale, vermouth, lime and fruit juices, and margarita and sour mixes
Garnishes	Lemons, limes, olives, onions, margarita salt, and bitters
Liquor	Vodka, gin, rum, scotch, blended whiskey, tequila, and bourbon
Wine	Red, white, and Champagne
Beer	Bottled light and dark
Barware	Corkscrew, bottle opener, sharp knife, cutting board, shaker, jigger, napkins, toothpicks, and glasses

Don't forget the ice!

For a party of more than twenty-five guests, it's a good idea to hire a bartender or ask a friend to pitch in.

Stocking the Bar

Party Starters

Beach Bites

8 ounces cream cheese, softened
2 tablespoons milk
$1/2$ teaspoon horseradish
1 tablespoon melted butter
1 tablespoon white wine (optional)
$1/4$ teaspoon salt
$1/4$ teaspoon pepper
1 cup flaked cooked crab meat, drained
2 scallions, chopped
1 cup cooked shrimp, cut into small pieces
40 frozen phyllo cups, thawed
Grated Parmesan cheese
Sliced almonds

Blend the cream cheese, milk, horseradish, butter, wine, salt and pepper in a mixing bowl. Fold in the crab meat, scallions and shrimp. Fill the phyllo cups with the seafood mixture. Place on a baking sheet. Sprinkle with the cheese and almonds. Bake at 400 degrees for 10 to 12 minutes or until heated through.

Makes 40

COCKTAILS

The easiest way to get a party started is to offer your guests a drink. One fun idea is to greet guests with a signature cocktail that sets the stage for the evening. Meet guests at the door with sake for an Asian-inspired night or bellinis to remember a trip to Italy. Pink cosmopolitans are an obvious choice for Valentine's Day, but why not mix it up and serve your sweetie an "old-fashioned" to celebrate all the years of love you have shared.

Hot out of the oven, this bubbling cheese and crab combination will make your mouth water.

Crab Tartlets

TARTLET SHELLS

1 cup (2 sticks) butter, softened
6 ounces cream cheese, softened
2 cups flour
1 teaspoon salt

CRAB FILLING

1 pound crab meat (preferably fresh back fin)
8 ounces sharp Cheddar cheese, shredded
$1/2$ cup mayonnaise
1 small onion, chopped
4 green onions, finely chopped

For the shells, cream the butter and cream cheese in a mixing bowl until light and fluffy. Stir in the flour and salt. Shape into 48 balls. Chill for 1 hour. Press the pastry into greased miniature muffin cups. Set aside.

For the filling, combine the crab meat, cheese, mayonnaise, onion and green onions in a bowl and mix well. Spoon the filling into the shells. Bake at 350 degrees for 30 minutes or until golden brown and bubbly.

Makes 48

The basil aïoli gives this traditional Florida appetizer a unique twist.

Crab Cakes on Toast Points

BASIL AÏOLI

3/4 cup mayonnaise
1/3 cup finely chopped fresh basil
1 tablespoon fresh lemon juice

1 1/2 teaspoons lemon zest
1 1/2 teaspoons minced garlic
Salt and pepper to taste

CRAB CAKES AND ASSEMBLY

1 egg, beaten
2 1/2 tablespoons chopped fresh
   Italian parsley
1 1/2 tablespoons chopped scallions
1 tablespoon minced red bell pepper
1 1/2 tablespoons stone-ground
   mustard with seeds
1/4 teaspoon Worcestershire sauce
1/2 habanero chile, seeded and minced

1/4 cup mayonnaise
Juice of 1 lime
Salt and pepper to taste
1 pound fresh lump crab meat, flaked
1/2 cup (about) fresh bread crumbs
2 tablespoons (or more) butter
1 loaf French bread, cut diagonally into
   8 (3/4-inch) slices

For the aïoli, combine the mayonnaise, basil, lemon juice, lemon zest, garlic, salt and pepper in a small bowl and mix well. Chill, covered, for 1 hour to 2 days.

For the crab cakes and assembly, mix the egg, parsley, scallions, bell pepper, mustard, Worcestershire sauce, habanero chile, mayonnaise, lime juice, salt and pepper in a large bowl. Gently stir in the crab meat, breaking up the crab meat as little as possible. Gently stir in 1/4 cup of the bread crumbs. Add just enough of the remaining bread crumbs for the mixture to hold together. Shape into 8 cakes. Chill, covered, for 30 minutes or longer. Melt 2 tablespoons butter in a skillet over medium heat. Fry the crab cakes in the butter for 1 minute per side or until golden brown, adding additional butter to the skillet if needed; use 2 forks to turn the crab cakes. Drain on paper towels. Place the crab cakes on a baking sheet and keep warm. Lightly toast the French bread. Place 1 crab cake on each toast point. Top with a spoonful of the aïoli. Drizzle the remaining aïoli onto the serving plates.

Makes 8

It's all in the hearts, artichoke and palm, married to Florida shrimp. Ideal for brunch or luncheon.

Shrimp with Artichokes

2 pounds cooked shrimp, peeled
2 (14-ounce) cans artichoke hearts, drained
1 small to medium onion, separated into thin rings
1 (14-ounce) can hearts of palm, drained
1 cup vegetable oil
$1/2$ cup vinegar
$1/2$ cup dry white wine
1 tablespoon chopped fresh parsley
1 teaspoon sugar
1 teaspoon dried cilantro
$1/2$ teaspoon salt
$1/2$ teaspoon paprika
$1/4$ teaspoon whole black peppercorns
1 garlic clove, minced

Place the shrimp, artichoke hearts, onion and hearts of palm in a 4-quart container.
Mix the oil, vinegar, white wine, parsley, sugar, cilantro, salt, paprika, peppercorns
and garlic in a large bowl. Pour over the shrimp mixture. Marinate, covered, in the
refrigerator for 8 to 10 hours, stirring occasionally.

Makes 6 servings

CHOOSING THE LOCATION

*Where to have your party is as open as when. How about in the park, on your front porch, or in your
child's playhouse? Be creative—you don't always have to seat dinner guests in the dining room. Perhaps
you forget the table altogether and sit on cushions on the floor around the coffee table. How about
your backyard? Your boat? You may even use your neighborhood cul de sac as a gathering place.
Possibilities abound.*

The pesto, pine nuts, and sweet hot mustard provide the tang for this chicken tart appetizer.

Chicken Pesto Tarts

2 (15-ounce) packages refrigerator pie pastry
5 or 6 large chicken breasts
Salt and pepper to taste
2 teaspoons olive oil
$1/4$ cup pesto
$3/4$ cup mayonnaise
5 or 6 celery hearts, chopped
1 tablespoon sweet hot mustard
$1/2$ teaspoon celery salt
Toasted pine nuts (optional) (see Note)

Unfold 1 pie pastry onto waxed paper. Press out the fold lines with a rolling pin. Cut with a $2^{1}/_{2}$-inch round fluted cookie cutter. Press the rounds into miniature muffin cups, trimming the edges if needed. Repeat with the remaining pastries. Freeze, covered, for 15 minutes. Bake the tart shells at 425 degrees for 6 to 8 minutes or until golden brown. Cool in the pan for 10 minutes. Remove the tart shells to a wire rack to cool completely.

Sprinkle the chicken with salt, pepper and olive oil. Place in a baking dish. Bake at 400 degrees for 20 to 25 minutes or until cooked through. Cool and coarsely chop. Place in a large bowl. Mix the pesto, mayonnaise, celery, mustard and celery salt in a bowl. Add the pesto mixture 1 tablespoon at a time to the chicken until it holds together and is the desired consistency. Spoon into the tart shells. Sprinkle with toasted pine nuts.

Note: The unbaked tart shells can be frozen for up to 2 weeks. To toast pine nuts, spread in nonstick ovenproof pan and bake at 425 degrees for 1 minute or until toasted. Watch carefully, as they burn easily.

Makes 54 to 60

Asparagus in Endive

TANGERINE MARINADE

1 tangerine
1/2 garlic clove, crushed
1/4 teaspoon salt
1/4 teaspoon pepper
2 teaspoons chopped fresh tarragon
1/2 teaspoon Dijon mustard
2 teaspoons honey
4 teaspoons olive oil

ASPARAGUS AND ASSEMBLY

20 small asparagus spears, trimmed
3 heads Belgian endive
8 ounces cream cheese, softened
3 slices prosciutto, cut into thin strips

For the marinade, use a zester to remove the tangerine zest in fine strips. Cut the tangerine into halves and squeeze the juice into a bowl. Add the garlic, salt, pepper, tarragon, mustard, honey and olive oil and mix well. Stir in the tangerine zest.

For the asparagus and assembly, fill a shallow skillet half full with water and bring to a boil. Add the asparagus. Cook for 3 to 4 minutes or until tender. Drain and cool. Cut the asparagus into 1-inch lengths and place in a shallow bowl. Pour the marinade over the asparagus. Chill, covered, for 1 hour or longer. Separate the endive into individual leaves. Cut each leaf into 1-inch lengths. Spread a small amount of cream cheese on each piece of endive. Top each with a piece of asparagus. Wrap a prosciutto strip around each leaf. Arrange on a platter and garnish with tangerine wedges and sprigs of fresh dill weed.

Makes 20

Miniature Onion Quiches

$3/4$ cup crushed saltine crackers
$1/4$ cup ($1/2$ stick) butter, melted
$1/2$ cup chopped Vidalia onion
$1/2$ cup chopped green onions
2 tablespoons butter
2 eggs, beaten
$1/2$ cup milk
$1/2$ cup heavy cream
$1/2$ teaspoon salt
$1/2$ teaspoon black pepper
$1/2$ teaspoon cayenne pepper
1 cup (4 ounces) shredded Gruyère or white Cheddar cheese

Combine the cracker crumbs and $1/4$ cup butter in a bowl and mix well. Pat into miniature muffin cups sprayed with nonstick cooking spray. Sauté the onion and green onions in 2 tablespoons butter in a skillet for 10 minutes. Cool slightly. Spoon the onion mixture into the muffin cups. Combine the eggs, milk, cream, salt, black pepper, cayenne pepper and cheese in a mixing bowl and mix well. Pour over the onion mixture, filling the muffin cups $3/4$ full. Bake at 300 degrees for 15 to 20 minutes or until heated through and golden brown on top.

Note: The quiches may be prepared in advance and refrigerated or frozen. Reheat before serving.

Makes 12

Roasted Red Potato Bites

12 small red potatoes
1 tablespoon olive oil
4 ounces cream cheese, softened
$1/2$ cup (2 ounces) shredded sharp Cheddar cheese
$1/2$ cup (2 ounces) shredded Swiss cheese
8 ounces bacon, crisp-cooked and crumbled
$1/2$ cup minced green onions
1 teaspoon thyme

Rub the potatoes with olive oil and place on a baking sheet. Bake at 400 degrees for 45 minutes or until tender; cool. Cut each potato into halves. If needed, cut a small slice off the bottom of each half for a base so the potatoes can sit level. Scoop the potato pulp into a large mixing bowl, leaving $1/4$-inch-thick shells. Set the shells aside. Add the cream cheese, Cheddar cheese, Swiss cheese, bacon, green onions and thyme to the potato pulp and mix well. Spoon or pipe the cheese mixture into the potato shells. Place on a lightly greased baking sheet. Broil 6 inches from the heat source for 3 to 5 minutes or until lightly browned. Garnish with sliced green onions.

Note: The potatoes may be refrigerated, covered, up to 2 days before broiling. Bring them to room temperature before broiling.

Makes 24

Stuffed Cherry Tomatoes

1 pint cherry tomatoes
4 slices bacon, crisp-cooked, crumbled

$^1/_2$ bunch green onions, finely chopped
$^1/_4$ cup mayonnaise

Cut a thin slice off the bottom of the tomatoes so they can stand upright. Cut the top $^1/_4$ of each tomato almost off. Scoop out the tomato pulp and seeds. Mix the bacon, green onions and mayonnaise and spoon into the tomatoes. Chill thoroughly.

Makes 12 servings

Black olives add a twist to this traditional bruschetta.

Savory Bruschetta

1 large loaf French bread
$^1/_4$ cup extra-virgin olive oil
1 garlic clove, minced
6 to 8 tomatoes, seeded and chopped
1 cup chopped red onion
3 garlic cloves, minced
25 fresh basil leaves, chopped

2 teaspoons kosher salt
2 teaspoons freshly ground pepper
$^1/_2$ cup extra-virgin olive oil
$^1/_4$ to $^1/_2$ cup balsamic vinegar, or to taste
8 ounces cream cheese, softened
3 tablespoons grated Parmesan cheese
2 tablespoons chopped pitted black olives

Cut the bread into 16 slices. Brush with a mixture of $^1/_4$ cup olive oil and 1 garlic clove. Place on a baking sheet. Bake at 400 degrees for 8 to 10 minutes or until crisp. Mix the tomatoes, red onion, 3 garlic cloves, basil, salt and pepper in a glass bowl. Pour a mixture of $^1/_2$ cup olive oil and vinegar over the tomato mixture and toss. Chill until needed. Blend the cheeses in a mixing bowl. Stir in the olives. Spread over the toast. Drain the tomato mixture and spoon over the cream cheese.

Makes 16

The tomato-infused vodka from the marinating process makes a delicious cocktail.

Tipsy Tomatoes

2 pints grape tomatoes
1 cup vodka
1 teaspoon salt

2 teaspoons each pepper and sugar
1 tablespoon vinegar
Horseradish (optional)

Blanch the tomatoes in boiling water for 1 to 2 minutes or until the peels split. Plunge into a bowl of ice water. Slip off the tomato peels. Place the tomatoes in a large bowl. Mix the vodka, salt, pepper, sugar, vinegar and horseradish in a small bowl. Pour over the tomatoes. Chill, covered, for 2 hours or longer. Drain well. Serve on wooden picks. Garnish with parsley.

Makes 20 servings

At the end of this cocktail you'll have the chance to say, "It's all over but the pickle."

Bloody Bulldawg

Ice
2 tablespoons juice from bread-and-butter pickles
1/2 teaspoon horseradish
3 shakes garlic salt
1/2 teaspoon Tabasco sauce, or to taste
1 teaspoon Worcestershire sauce

1 shot of lemon juice
4 shakes Old Bay seasoning
3 shakes pepper
6 ounces vegetable juice cocktail
2 ounces vodka, or to taste
1 bread-and-butter pickle slice

Spoon ice into a tall glass. Add the pickle juice, horseradish, garlic salt, Tabasco sauce, Worcestershire sauce, lemon juice, Old Bay seasoning, pepper, vegetable juice cocktail and vodka and mix well. Add the pickle slice.

Makes 1

Asiago Puffs

12 to 14 slices firm white bread,
  crusts removed
1/2 cup mayonnaise

1/4 cup minced onion
1/3 cup grated asiago cheese
2 scallions, cut into thin diagonal slices

Lightly toast the bread and cut into quarters. Combine the mayonnaise, onion and cheese in a small bowl and mix well. Spread a thin layer of the mayonnaise mixture over the toast squares. Arrange on a baking sheet. Broil 6 inches from the heat source for 30 seconds or until lightly browned and bubbly. Top with scallion slices.

Makes 48 to 56

Spread on cream cheese; serve with water crackers. Or, spoon over ice cream or angel food cake.

Strawberry Preserves

2 cups (about 1 pint) strawberries,
  trimmed and quartered
1 1/2 cups sugar

2 tablespoons red wine vinegar
2 tablespoons water
1 teaspoon cracked black pepper

Combine the strawberries, sugar, vinegar, water and pepper in a heavy medium saucepan. Bring to a boil, stirring constantly; skim the surface. Reduce the heat and simmer for 30 minutes or until thickened and translucent, stirring and skimming foam occasionally. Let cool completely.

Note: For storage, pour hot preserves into hot sterilized jars. Store in the refrigerator for up to 1 month. Frozen strawberries can be used in this recipe, but thaw and drain them first.

Makes 12 servings

Baked Brie en Croûte

1/4 cup packed light brown sugar
1/4 cup chopped walnuts
1 tablespoon bourbon
1 (8-count) can refrigerator crescent rolls
1 (10-ounce) round Brie cheese
1 egg, beaten

Combine the brown sugar, walnuts and bourbon in a bowl and mix well. Place in an airtight container and chill for 12 hours to 1 week. Unroll the crescent roll dough into a single sheet, pressing out the perforations. Place the cheese in the center of the dough. Spread with the walnut mixture. Bring up the sides of the dough to cover the cheese. Trim off any excess dough. Brush the top of the dough with the egg. Bake using the crescent roll package directions or until golden brown. Serve with apple slices and crackers.

Note: If desired, use seasonal cookie cutters to turn the dough scraps into decorative accents. Brush with some of the beaten egg and press onto the crust.

Makes 8 to 10 servings

SELECTING WINE

Drink what you like. The days of white wine with fish and poultry or red wine with red meat are passé. Find a professional you trust and ask for guidance. Always be willing to try something new!
—Chad Munsey

Shrimp Butter

$1/2$ cup (1 stick) margarine, softened
$1/4$ cup ($1/2$ stick) butter, softened
$1/4$ cup mayonnaise
Juice of 1 small lemon
8 ounces cream cheese, softened
1 tablespoon grated onion
Dash of Worcestershire sauce
Dash of hot sauce
Salt to taste
1 pound peeled cooked shrimp, finely chopped
Paprika (optional)
Sliced olives (optional)
Parsley (optional)

Combine the margarine, butter, mayonnaise, lemon juice, cream cheese, onion,
Worcestershire sauce, hot sauce and salt in a mixing bowl and beat until creamy.
Add the shrimp and mix well. Shape as desired. Sprinkle with paprika and decorate
with olives and parsley. Chill, covered, until serving time. Serve with crackers.

Makes 12 servings

Bleu Cheese Clam Dip

8 ounces cream cheese, softened
8 ounces bleu cheese, crumbled
2 (7-ounce) cans minced clams, drained

1 green onion, coarsely chopped
3 or 4 drops of hot sauce

Combine the cream cheese, bleu cheese, clams, green onions and hot sauce in a bowl and mix well. Serve with crackers or breadsticks.

Makes 10 servings

A fresh salsa for chips or an accompaniment to grilled chicken or fish.

Mango and Corn Salsa

$1^1/2$ cups fresh corn kernels
   (about 3 ears)
1 teaspoon vegetable oil
$1^1/2$ cups chopped peeled mango
$1/4$ cup fresh lemon juice or lime juice

2 tablespoons chopped sweet onion
2 tablespoons minced fresh mint
2 tablespoons minced fresh cilantro
$1^1/2$ teaspoons grated peeled gingerroot
$1/4$ teaspoon salt

Combine the corn kernels and oil in a bowl and toss to coat. Spread the corn on a baking sheet. Bake at 400 degrees for 15 minutes; let cool. Combine the corn, mango, lemon juice, onion, mint, cilantro, gingerroot and salt in a bowl and toss gently.

Makes 6 to 8 servings

The perfect First Coast cooler for any outdoor summer event.

Ortega Lemonade

4 gallons lemonade

8 (12-ounce) cans frozen lemonade
concentrate, thawed

4 (12-ounce) cans frozen limeade
concentrate, thawed

4 (16-ounce) bottles Key lime juice

6 (1.75-liter) bottles citrus-flavored
vodka

10 each lemons and limes, sliced

Ice

Combine the first 5 ingredients in a 48-quart cooler. Mix well with a wooden spoon. Add the lemon and lime slices. Add enough ice to fill the cooler 2/3 full. Fill the cooler to the top with water. Mix well. Pour over ice in tall glasses. Serve with straws.

Makes 50 servings

This extra-dry Spanish sparkling wine makes the perfect light drink for a brunch or luncheon.

Cava Sangria

1 bottle Cava wine

1 cup lemon juice

2 cups sparkling white grape juice

2 cups sweetened pineapple juice

3 cups lemon-lime soda

1 lemon, sliced

Mix the ingredients in a large pitcher. Chill until cold or pour into a large glass punch bowl with ice. Garnish with pineapple slices, pineapple chunks or sliced strawberries.

Makes 24 servings

SWEET SPARKLER

Rim a glass with pasteurized egg white, dip it in colored sugar to match your party theme, then let it dry. You'll add to your party's sparkle and give every guest a sweet treat.

The mulling of the spices will scent your room, while the rum will warm your guests.

Spiced Cranberry Tea Punch

4 cups cold water
4 tea bags
2 cups water
2 cups white or red grape juice
2 cups cranberry juice cocktail
$^1/_2$ cup sugar
$^1/_2$ teaspoon ground cinnamon
$^1/_4$ teaspoon allspice
$^1/_8$ teaspoon ground cloves
1 lemon, sliced
1 orange, sliced
1 lime, sliced
1 cup rum or whiskey (optional)

Bring the cold water to a boil in a 4-quart Dutch oven. Remove from the heat. Add the tea bags and steep for 3 to 5 minutes; discard the tea bags. Add the water, grape juice, cranberry juice cocktail, sugar, cinnamon, allspice and cloves. Return to a boil. Reduce the heat and simmer for 15 minutes. Add the lemon, orange and lime slices. Chill, covered, for 4 hours. Strain into a serving pitcher or punch bowl if desired. Serve the tea over ice in tall clear glasses. Garnish glasses with lemon, orange and/or lime slices. For a warm punch, pour the cranberry tea into a slow cooker. Add the rum and heat for 1 hour or longer. Serve in glass mugs or cups and garnish with cinnamon sticks or orange slices studded with whole cloves.

Makes 10 servings

Main
Events

Chef Victor P. Jones of Sterling's of Avondale shares one of his favorite classic grouper recipes.

Cornmeal-Crusted Grouper

GROUPER

4 (8-ounce) grouper, tilapia, salmon or flounder filets
1¹/₂ cups yellow cornmeal
Salt and pepper to taste
1 tablespoon cumin
3 tablespoons vegetable oil

OKRA TOMATO RAGOUT

1 pound fresh okra, cut into 1-inch rounds
1 small red or Bermuda onion, finely chopped
4 large garlic cloves, coarsely chopped
¹/₂ bunch fresh cilantro, coarsely chopped
3 tomatoes, cut into ¹/₂-inch pieces
¹/₂ cup fish stock or shrimp stock
¹/₄ cup (¹/₂ stick) butter, cut into pieces

For the grouper, coat the grouper in a mixture of the cornmeal, salt, pepper and cumin. Heat the oil in a large nonstick skillet over high heat. Add the grouper. Cook for 1¹/₂ to 2 minutes per side. Set the skillet aside. Remove the grouper to a baking sheet. Bake at 350 degrees for 10 to 12 minutes.

For the ragout, place the okra and onion in the skillet used for cooking the fish. Sauté until tender. Add the garlic, cilantro and tomatoes. Sauté for 3 minutes. Add the fish stock and bring to a boil. Reduce the heat to low. Add the butter and simmer for 5 to 7 minutes.

To serve, arrange the grouper on dinner plates. Spoon the ragout over the fish. Serve with yellow rice or grits.

Makes 4 servings

Horseradish-Crusted Salmon

1 pound salmon filet
$1/4$ teaspoon salt
$1/4$ teaspoon freshly ground pepper
$1/4$ cup prepared horseradish
1 egg
$1/2$ teaspoon thyme
$1/2$ teaspoon parsley
1 cup Italian-seasoned bread crumbs
1 cup flour
1 egg, beaten
3 tablespoons olive oil

Season the salmon with the salt and pepper. Combine the horseradish, 1 egg, thyme, parsley and bread crumbs in a bowl and mix well. Dust the salmon with flour. Dip the salmon in the beaten egg to coat. Press the horseradish mixture onto the salmon. Heat the olive oil in an ovenproof skillet until hot. Add the salmon to the skillet bread crumb side down. Cook for 30 seconds. Bake at 350 degrees for 8 to 10 minutes.

Makes 4 servings

STORING WINE

Not all wine is fine wine. Vintage dates for white wines are two to three years, and most red wines are four to six. There are always exceptions to the rules. If in doubt, drink it young.

—Chad Munsey

Olive and Caper Salsa adds a Mediterranean flair to Florida snapper.

Snapper with Caper Salsa

SNAPPER

4 (6-ounce) snapper filets
2 tablespoons olive oil
Salt and pepper to taste

OLIVE AND CAPER SALSA

1 tablespoon olive oil
1 tablespoon finely chopped shallot
$1/4$ teaspoon minced garlic
1 tablespoon balsamic vinegar
2 cups chopped seeded tomatoes
1 tablespoon capers
$1^1/2$ teaspoons chopped kalamata olives
$1/2$ teaspoon chopped fresh thyme
Salt and freshly ground pepper to taste

For the snapper, brush the filets with olive oil. Season with salt and pepper. Grill over hot coals until the fish flakes easily.

For the salsa, heat the olive oil in a sauté pan. Add the shallot and garlic. Sauté for 30 seconds. Add the vinegar, tomatoes, capers, olives and thyme. Simmer for 3 minutes. Season with salt and pepper. Serve over the snapper.

Makes 4 servings

Tuna with Mango Relish

MANGO RELISH
2 very ripe mangoes
1 ripe avocado
$1/2$ cup chopped fresh cilantro
$1/4$ cup chopped red onion or green onions

TUNA
$1/4$ cup soy sauce
$1/4$ cup teriyaki sauce
2 teaspoons chopped fresh gingerroot
2 teaspoons chopped garlic
4 medium tuna steaks

For the relish, cut the mangoes and avocado into $1/4$-inch chunks. Combine the mangoes, avocado, cilantro and onion in a bowl and mix well.

For the tuna, mix the soy sauce, teriyaki sauce, gingerroot and garlic in a shallow pan. Add the tuna and turn several times to coat. Marinate, covered, in the refrigerator for 1 hour. Remove the tuna and discard the marinade. Place the tuna on a grill rack or in a pan on top of the stove and cook for 2 to 3 minutes per side. Serve the tuna topped with the relish.

Makes 4 servings

Sesame Ginger Ahi Tuna

SESAME GINGER DRESSING

3 ounces fresh gingerroot,
    coarsely chopped
1 1/2 ounces garlic
1 bunch scallions
1 bunch cilantro

1/2 cup soy sauce
3/4 cup rice vinegar
1/2 cup sesame oil
1 1/2 cups peanut oil

TUNA

1 pound sashimi-grade ahi or
    yellowfin tuna
Salt to taste
2 cups peanut oil for deep frying
12 won ton wrappers

1 tablespoon sambal oelek (see Note)
1 pint daikon sprouts (see Note)
6 ounces pickled ginger
Black and white sesame seeds

For the dressing, combine the gingerroot, garlic, scallions, cilantro, soy sauce, vinegar and sesame oil in a food processor fitted with a steel blade. Process until minced. Add the peanut oil in a fine stream, processing constantly until emulsified. This dressing is also great on salads and grilled fish.

Note: Combined with mayonnaise, this dressing makes a fantastic crudité dip.

For the tuna, cut the tuna into 1/4-inch cubes. Season with salt and set aside. Heat the peanut oil to 350 degrees in a deep pan. Add the won ton wrappers and cook until crisp. Toss the tuna with the sesame ginger dressing. Place 1 to 2 ounces of the tuna mixture on each won ton wrapper. Stack 3 won tons on each serving plate. Top with sambal oelek, daikon sprouts, pickled ginger and sesame seeds.

Note: Sambal oelek is a condiment of chiles, brown sugar and salt. Daikon is an Asian radish. Both can be found in many large supermarkets and in international markets.

Makes 4 servings

Amelia Island Shrimp

Salt to taste
1 tablespoon olive oil
24 ounces linguini
6 tablespoons butter or margarine
6 tablespoons extra-virgin olive oil
10 garlic cloves, minced
2 pounds large shrimp, peeled
  and deveined
6 green onions, green tops chopped,
  white bulbs sliced
1^1/2 teaspoons salt

^{1}/2 teaspoon black pepper
1 cup finely chopped fresh parsley
^{1}/2 cup fresh lemon juice
^{1}/2 cup white wine
^{1}/4 cup chopped fresh basil
^{1}/2 to ^{3}/4 teaspoon hot red pepper flakes
1 cup (4 ounces) grated Parmigiano-
  Reggiano cheese
Lemon wedges
Parsley sprigs

Bring a large stockpot of salted water to a boil. Add 1 tablespoon olive oil. Add the pasta and cook until al dente; drain and keep warm.

Melt the butter with 6 tablespoons olive oil in a large sauté pan. Add the garlic. Sauté over low heat for 1 minute; do not burn. Increase the heat to medium. Add the shrimp, green onion bulbs, 1^1/2 teaspoons salt and black pepper. Sauté just until the shrimp curl and turn pink. Add the parsley, lemon juice, wine, basil and red pepper flakes and mix well. Cook until heated through.

Remove the pasta to a large serving platter or individual bowls. Pour the shrimp and sauce over the pasta. Sprinkle with the cheese and green onion tops. Garnish with lemon wedges and sprigs of fresh parsley.

For scallop scampi, substitute 2 pounds scallops for the shrimp. Sauté until the scallops are tender and the edges are beginning to turn caramel-colored.

Makes 6 servings

Grilled Soft-Shell Crab

FENNEL SALAD

1 small shallot, minced
Butter
2 tablespoons Champagne vinegar
2 sprigs of fresh rosemary,
    finely chopped

3/4 cup mild olive oil
Kosher salt and pepper to taste
1 fennel bulb, cored and shaved
    very thin
Peel of 1 tomato, julienned

ORANGE AÏOLI

1 egg yolk (see Note)
Juice of 1 blood orange
1 cup mild olive oil

1 garlic clove, minced
Butter
Salt and pepper to taste

CRAB

4 soft-shell crabs, cleaned
1/4 cup mild olive oil

Kosher salt and pepper to taste

For the salad, cook the shallot in a small amount of butter in a saucepan until tender but not browned. Whisk the shallot, vinegar, rosemary and olive oil in a bowl. Season with salt and pepper. Add the fennel and tomato peel and toss to mix.

For the aïoli, whisk the egg yolk and some of the orange juice in a bowl. Add the olive oil in a fine stream, whisking constantly until of mayonnaise consistency. Cook the garlic in butter in a saucepan until tender but not browned. Stir the cooked garlic and remaining orange juice into the aïoli. Season with salt and pepper.

For the crab, brush each crab with olive oil and season with salt and pepper. Grill over medium heat. Spoon the aïoli onto a serving plate. Top with the crab. Place the fennel salad on the crab, keeping it high and tight. Garnish with blood orange segments.

Note: To avoid using raw egg yolks, use yolks from eggs pasteurized in their shells, which are sold at some specialty food stores, or an equivalent amount of pasteurized egg substitute.

Makes 4 servings

Sautéed garlic and onion marinated inside the beef filet make for flavor perfection.

Garlic-Stuffed Filets

1 tablespoon olive oil
1 tablespoon butter
$1/4$ cup finely chopped garlic
$1/2$ cup thinly sliced green onions

$1/2$ teaspoon salt
$1/2$ teaspoon pepper
2 tablespoons Worcestershire sauce
4 (2-inch-thick) beef filets

Heat the olive oil and butter in a small skillet over low heat. Add the garlic and sauté until tender. Add the green onions and cook for 5 minutes or until tender. Add the salt, pepper and Worcestershire sauce. Let cool. Cut a pocket in the side of each filet, cutting to but not through the opposite side. Spread the garlic mixture evenly in the pocket. Secure the opening with wooden picks. Chill, covered, in the refrigerator for several hours to overnight. Grill the filets over medium-low heat to desired degree of doneness.

Makes 4 servings

The perfect blend of cheeses and cream in this rich sauce melts with each bite of filet.

Filets with Gorgonzola

$3^1/2$ cups heavy cream
3 ounces Gorgonzola cheese, shredded
2 tablespoons grated asiago cheese
$1/2$ teaspoon salt

$1/2$ teaspoon pepper
3 tablespoons minced fresh parsley
6 (8-ounce) beef filets

Bring the heavy cream to a boil in a medium saucepan over medium-high heat. Boil rapidly for 45 minutes or until thickened, stirring occasionally. Remove from the heat. Whisk in the cheese, salt, pepper and parsley. Keep warm over low heat. Grill the filets to the desired degree of doneness. Pour the gorgonzola sauce over the filets.

Makes 6 servings

Serve with Avocado Papaya Chill (page 75) for an exotic island-themed event.

Tropical Steak

¹/4 cup Caribbean jerk seasoning
4 New York strip steaks
¹/4 cup soy sauce

¹/4 cup pineapple juice
2 tablespoons minced garlic

Rub 1 tablespoon jerk seasoning on 1 side of each steak. Place in a shallow dish. Mix the remaining ingredients in a bowl. Pour over the steaks. Marinate, covered, in the refrigerator for 2 hours or longer. Grill the steaks to the desired degree of doneness. To serve as an appetizer, cut the steaks into bite-size pieces and serve on skewers.

Makes 4 servings

A great portable gourmet lunch that's perfect for game-day tailgating.

London Broil Sandwiches

1 (2-pound) London broil
2 tablespoons vegetable oil
2 teaspoons dried parsley
2 tablespoons Worcestershire sauce
1 garlic clove, minced
1 teaspoon each salt and lemon juice

¹/2 teaspoon pepper
Prepared pesto
1 loaf sourdough bread, sliced
   and toasted
Red onion, sliced
Arugula

Place the beef in a foil-lined 9×13-inch baking pan. Whisk the next 7 ingredients in a small bowl. Pour over the beef. Marinate, covered with plastic wrap, in the refrigerator for 24 to 48 hours, turning occasionally. Remove the plastic wrap. Broil 2 inches from the heat source for 5 to 7 minutes per side for medium rare. Let stand for 5 minutes. Using an electric knife, slice on the grain as thinly as possible. Spread pesto on each bread slice. Layer the beef, onion slices and arugula on the bread. Serve warm or cold.

Makes 8 servings

Raspberry Chicken

4 boneless skinless chicken breasts
Salt to taste
Flour
2 tablespoons butter
$1/4$ cup finely chopped shallot
3 tablespoons raspberry jam or jelly
3 tablespoons raspberry vinegar or red wine vinegar
$1/4$ cup heavy cream

Season the chicken with salt and dust lightly with flour. Melt the butter in a large sauté pan. Add the chicken and cook over medium heat for 5 minutes per side. Add the shallot. Cook for 5 minutes longer. Remove the chicken and keep warm.

Add the jam and vinegar to the sauté pan. Cook briefly, stirring frequently to loosen any browned bits in the pan. Bring to a boil. Boil for 1 minute or until the liquid is slightly reduced. Stir in the cream and bring to a boil. Pour over the chicken. Garnish with fresh raspberries.

Makes 4 servings

Warm or cold, this yummy, simple pesto chicken and pasta dish is great for those days on the go.

Chicken Pesto with Bow Ties

16 ounces bow tie pasta
1 cooked rotisserie chicken, boned and cut into bite-size pieces
1 cup (4 ounces) grated asiago cheese
1 cup (4 ounces) grated Parmesan cheese
1 (8-ounce) jar prepared pesto
1 cup pine nuts
Sun-dried tomatoes

Cook the pasta using the package directions until al dente; drain. Remove the chicken from the bones. Toss the pasta, chicken, Parmesan cheese, asiago cheese, pesto and pine nuts in a large serving bowl. Top with sun-dried tomatoes. Serve hot as a main dish with garlic bread and Caesar salad, or serve cold as a picnic salad.

Makes 6 servings

INVITATIONS

Think outside the envelope! For a pool party, try writing the information on an inexpensive beach ball, then deflate and send it in a brightly colored box. Perhaps a fiesta could be announced on a mini sombrero. Or for a bridal tea, attach a handwritten card to an actual tea bag. A note pinned to a gardening glove sets the stage for a fun and casual gathering in the garden.

Bruschetta Chicken

8 ounces angel hair pasta
4 boneless skinless chicken breasts
1 teaspoon olive oil
1 onion, chopped
5 garlic cloves, minced
1 tablespoon Italian seasoning blend
1 tablespoon red pepper flakes
3 tomatoes, chopped
1^1/$_2$ cups sliced white mushrooms
^{1}/$_4$ cup torn fresh basil leaves
1 teaspoon olive oil

Cook the pasta using the package directions until al dente; drain. Set aside. Grill the chicken until cooked through. Set aside. Heat 1 teaspoon olive oil in a large skillet. Add the onion and garlic. Sauté for 4 minutes or until tender. Add the Italian seasoning blend, red pepper flakes and tomatoes. Sauté for 2 minutes or until softened. Add the mushrooms, basil, 1 teaspoon olive oil and chicken. Simmer over medium heat for 5 minutes. Serve the chicken and sauce over the pasta.

Makes 4 servings

Grilled Rosemary Garlic

LAMB

2 tablespoons finely chopped
   fresh rosemary
4 garlic cloves, finely chopped
1 1/2 cups high-quality extra-virgin
   olive oil

2 (8-bone) domestic lamb racks,
   Frenched and fat removed
Kosher salt
Freshly ground pepper

ASIAGO SEMOLINA POLENTA

2 cups chicken stock or low-sodium
   chicken broth
1 1/2 cups heavy cream

1 cup semolina
1/2 teaspoon kosher salt
1/2 cup (2 ounces) grated asiago cheese

RADICCHIO TREVISO

2 tablespoons balsamic vinegar
3 tablespoons extra-virgin olive oil
Pinch of kosher salt

Pinch of freshly ground pepper
1 head radicchio di Treviso (long-leaf
   radicchio), quartered lengthwise

MINT GREMOLATA

1 tablespoon finely chopped toasted
   pine nuts
1 teaspoon grated lemon zest
1 1/2 tablespoons dry bread crumbs

1 1/2 tablespoons finely chopped
   fresh mint
Pinch of kosher salt
Pinch of freshly ground pepper

For the lamb, mix the rosemary, garlic and olive oil in a bowl. Cut the lamb racks into 2-bone chops. Add to the olive oil mixture. Marinate, covered, in the refrigerator for 12 hours; drain and discard the marinade. Season the lamb chops with salt and pepper. Wrap the Frenched parts with foil. Grill over high heat just long enough to make grill marks on each side. Remove from the grill and place the lamb chops in a roasting pan. Bake at 350 degrees to cook to desired degree of doneness.

Lamb Chops

For the polenta, combine the chicken stock and heavy cream in a heavy saucepan and bring to a simmer. Whisk in the semolina and salt. Cook over very low heat until the semolina is soft, stirring frequently. Whisk in the cheese. Keep warm over very low heat.

For the radicchio, whisk the balsamic vinegar, olive oil, salt and pepper in a bowl. Add the radicchio and toss. Grill just until grill marks form and the leaves are wilted.

For the gremolata, combine the pine nuts, lemon zest, bread crumbs, mint, salt and pepper in a bowl and mix well.

To serve, place the polenta slightly off center on a serving plate. Arrange interlocking lamb chop bones in front of the polenta. Place the radicchio on top of the polenta, leaning against the lamb chops. Sprinkle the gremolata liberally over the lamb chops.

Makes 4 servings

SERVING WINE

Keep it simple. White wine should always be served chilled. Champagne and other sparkling wines, sauvignon blanc, and pinot grigio are best served ice-cold. Dispel the myth of red wine served at room temperature. Five hundred years ago, everyone lived in castles, which had a room temperature of sixty degrees—not so likely in Florida. As a general rule, place red wine in the refrigerator fifteen minutes before serving.

—Chad Munsey

Peppercorn Pork Tenderloin

^{1}/4 cup Worcestershire sauce
^{1}/4 cup low-sodium soy sauce
^{1}/4 cup dry white wine
1 tablespoon honey
^{1}/2 teaspoon nutmeg
3 large garlic cloves, minced
1 (2^1/2-pound) pork tenderloin
Coarsely ground black peppercorns

Combine the Worcestershire sauce, soy sauce, wine, honey, nutmeg and garlic in a sealable plastic bag. Add the pork. Seal the bag and shake to coat the pork. Marinate in the refrigerator for 6 to 8 hours, turning twice. Remove the pork from the marinade, discarding the marinade.

Spread the peppercorns on a piece of parchment paper laid over waxed paper. Roll the pork in the peppercorns. Sear all sides of the pork in a heavy skillet. Place the pork in a baking pan. Bake at 350 degrees for 1 hour or until a meat thermometer inserted into the thickest part of the pork registers 160 degrees. Let stand for 10 minutes before slicing.

Makes 8 servings

Pair with Butternut Squash Soup (page 74) and Caramel Baked Apples (page 105).

Pork with Apple Chutney

APPLE ONION CHUTNEY

1/4 cup olive oil

4 onions, thinly sliced

1/3 cup balsamic vinegar

1/3 cup sherry vinegar

2 small Granny Smith apples, peeled, cored and cut into 1/2-inch pieces

2 tablespoons yellow mustard seeds

1 tablespoon sugar

1/2 teaspoon ginger

1/2 teaspoon ground allspice

PORK

1 (4- to 41/3-pound) center-cut pork loin

Salt and pepper to taste

2 tablespoons butter

1 tablespoon olive oil

11/4 cups low-sodium chicken broth

For the chutney, heat the olive oil in a heavy skillet over medium-high heat. Add the onions. Sauté for 30 minutes or until golden brown. Stir in the balsamic vinegar and sherry vinegar. Add the apples, mustard seeds, sugar, ginger and allspice. Reduce the heat to medium. Sauté for 15 minutes or until the apples are tender.

For the pork, season the pork loin with salt and pepper. Heat the butter with the olive oil in a large wide Dutch oven over medium-high heat until the butter melts and begins to brown. Add the pork. Cook for 8 minutes or until brown on all sides. Add 3/4 cup of the chicken broth. Bake, covered, at 375 degrees for 35 minutes or until a meat thermometer inserted into the thickest portion of the pork registers 160 degrees. Remove the pork to a platter. Cover with a tent of foil and set aside. Pour the cooking liquid into a cup. Freeze for 5 minutes. Spoon off and discard all but 1 tablespoon fat. Return the cooking liquid to the Dutch oven. Add Apple Onion Chutney and remaining 1/2 cup chicken broth. Simmer for 4 minutes to blend the flavors. Season with salt and pepper. Slice the pork and spoon chutney over it.

Makes 10 to 12 servings

Tolomato Chili

8 ounces dried black beans
1 habanero chile, seeded and chopped
3 onions, chopped
6 garlic cloves, minced
1 tablespoon olive oil
2 bay leaves
Salt and pepper to taste
1¹/2 pounds spicy Italian sausage,
    casings removed
1 teaspoon each cumin and coriander
1 tablespoon olive oil
1 yellow bell pepper, diced

1 jalapeño chile, seeded and chopped
1 tablespoon olive oil
2 tablespoons chili powder
1 teaspoon cinnamon
1 (28-ounce) can whole tomatoes
1 tomato, seeded and coarsely chopped
1 (12-ounce) bottle beer
1 (14-ounce) can diced tomatoes
1 tomato, seeded and coarsely chopped
¹/2 bunch cilantro, coarsely chopped
Sour cream
Shredded cheese

Sort and rinse the beans. Soak in water to cover for 12 hours; drain well. Chop the onions and mince the garlic. Divide each into 3 equal portions. Sauté the habanero chile, 1 chopped onion and 2 minced garlic cloves in 1 tablespoon olive oil in a saucepan until the onion is tender. Add the beans, bay leaves and water to cover. Simmer until the beans are soft but still intact. Season with salt and pepper. Set aside.

Sauté the sausage in a skillet, stirring until crumbly. Add the cumin, coriander, salt and pepper. Add 1 tablespoon olive oil. Add the bell pepper, jalapeño chile, 1 chopped onion and 2 minced garlic cloves. Cook until the sausage is lightly browned. Heat 1 tablespoon olive oil in a large saucepan. Add 1 chopped onion and 2 minced garlic cloves. Sauté until the onion is tender. Add the chili powder, cinnamon, salt and pepper, canned tomatoes and 1 coarsely chopped tomato. Cook until the mixture is the consistency of chunky tomato sauce. Combine the beans, sausage and tomatoes in one large stockpot. Add the beer. Add the canned diced tomatoes if the mixture is too thick or spicy. Simmer for 1 hour. Add 1 chopped tomato and the cilantro 15 minutes before serving. Discard the bay leaves. Top each serving with sour cream and cheese. This chili is even better served a day after it is prepared. Add the tomato and cilantro once the chili is reheated.

Makes 6 to 8 servings

Grilled Vegetable Sandwich

$1/2$ cup plus 2 tablespoons olive oil
2 garlic cloves, minced
2 small eggplant, cut into $1/4$-inch slices
Salt to taste
2 red bell peppers, sliced
$1/4$ teaspoon salt
$1/2$ teaspoon thyme
French bread
1 cup (4 ounces) shredded mozzarella cheese

Brush 2 baking sheets with olive oil. Mix the remaining olive oil and garlic in a bowl. Arrange the eggplant slices on the prepared baking sheet. Brush with some of the garlic oil. Sprinkle with salt. Bake at 450 degrees for 10 minutes. Combine the bell peppers, 1 tablespoon garlic oil and $1/4$ teaspoon salt. Turn the eggplant slices over. Arrange the bell pepper slices on the baking sheet. Sprinkle the vegetables with thyme. Bake at 450 degrees for 15 to 20 minutes or until the vegetables are very tender. Cut the bread into 4 pieces; split open. Brush the bread with the remaining garlic oil. Broil the bread 6 inches from the heat source until golden brown. Remove from the broiler. Top the bread with eggplant, bell peppers and cheese. Return to the broiler. Broil until the cheese melts.

Makes 4 servings

On the Side

You decide: is it the bacon or the sweet sherry that makes this memorable?

Corn and Crab Bisque

3 slices bacon, chopped
$1/2$ cup chopped onion
$1/2$ cup chopped celery
$2/3$ cup chopped mixed red and green bell peppers
2 tablespoons flour
3 cups hot chicken stock
2 cups milk
$1/4$ cup sweet sherry
2 cups corn (see Note)
$1/2$ teaspoon salt
$1/2$ teaspoon pepper
1 tablespoon sugar
Dash of Tabasco sauce
8 ounces crab meat, flaked
Chopped fresh herbs to taste

Cook the bacon in a large stockpot until crisp; reserve the drippings. Drain the bacon and set aside. Sauté the onion, celery and bell peppers in the drippings over medium heat until softened. Stir in the flour. Cook for 1 minute, stirring constantly. Add the chicken stock and cook for 2 to 3 minutes. Add the milk. Reduce the heat to low. Add the sherry, corn, salt, pepper, sugar and Tabasco sauce. Cook over low heat for 20 minutes. Stir in the crab meat. Sprinkle with the bacon and herbs.

Note: Use any type of corn—fresh, canned or frozen; whole kernel or creamed.

Makes 8 servings

This savory version of the classic bistro dish is an old family favorite.

French Onion Soup

5 tablespoons butter
4 to 5 pounds onions, thinly sliced
1/4 teaspoon pepper
2 tablespoons flour
5 (10-ounce) cans beef broth
5 cups water
2 bay leaves
Salt and pepper to taste (optional)
10 to 12 slices French bread
5 tablespoons grated Parmesan cheese
2 cups (8 ounces) shredded Gruyère cheese or Swiss cheese

Melt the butter in a 5-quart saucepan over high heat. Add the onions and pepper. Sauté until the onions are light golden brown. Sprinkle with the flour and stir until absorbed. Cook for 1 minute longer, stirring constantly with a wooden spoon. Remove from the heat. Add the beef broth to the onion mixture gradually, stirring constantly. Stir in the water and bay leaves. Bring the soup to a boil over medium-high heat, stirring constantly. Reduce the heat to low and simmer for 30 to 40 minutes. Add the salt and pepper. Discard the bay leaves. Ladle the soup into 8 heatproof soup bowls. Place on a baking sheet or in a large baking dish. Toast the bread slices light golden brown. Place the toast on the onion soup. Sprinkle liberally with the Parmesan cheese and Gruyère cheese. Broil the soup 6 inches from the heat source until the cheese melts and is golden brown. Serve immediately.

Makes 8 servings

Serve this vibrant sunset-colored soup for a first course your guests will remember.

Butternut Squash Soup

2 (2-pound) acorn squash
2 (2-pound) butternut squash
1/2 cup (1 stick) butter
8 teaspoons dark brown sugar
3 carrots, halved
1 large onion, thinly sliced
10 cups chicken broth
3/4 teaspoon mace
3/4 teaspoon ginger
Pinch of cayenne pepper
Salt to taste
Crème fraîche
Chopped chives

Cut the acorn squash and butternut squash lengthwise into halves and remove the seeds. Place the squash halves skin side down in a large baking pan. Place 1 tablespoon butter and 1 teaspoon brown sugar in each squash cavity. Arrange the carrots and onion around the squash. Add 2 cups of the chicken broth. Cover the pan tightly with foil. Bake at 350 degrees for 2 hours. Let the vegetables cool for 5 minutes. Scoop out the squash pulp and discard the skins. Place the squash, carrots, onion and cooking liquid in a large stockpot. Add the remaining 8 cups chicken broth, mace, ginger, cayenne pepper and salt and mix well. Bring to a boil; reduce the heat and simmer for 10 minutes. Purée the soup using an immersion blender, blender or food processor. Return the soup to the stockpot. Adjust the seasonings and cook until heated through. Ladle into bowls. Top each serving with a dollop of crème fraîche and a sprinkling of chives.

Makes 12 servings

Avocado Papaya Chill

1 cup unsweetened pineapple juice
2 tablespoons vegetable oil
3 tablespoons chili sauce
Juice of 2 limes
$1/4$ teaspoon nutmeg

$1/4$ teaspoon each salt and white pepper
2 large ripe avocados, sliced
2 ripe papaya, seeded and sliced
4 slices bacon, crisp-cooked
    and crumbled

Combine the pineapple juice, oil, chili sauce, lime juice, nutmeg, salt and white pepper in a bowl and mix well. Combine the avocado slices and papaya slices in a bowl. Pour the pineapple juice mixture over the fruit. Chill, covered, for 1 hour. Spoon into small bowls and sprinkle with the bacon.

Makes 8 to 12 servings

Riverfront Salad

1 (6-ounce) jar marinated artichoke
    hearts, drained, liquid reserved
1 very large head romaine
    lettuce, chopped
1 ripe avocado, chopped
2 green onions, chopped

2 or 3 ribs celery, chopped
1 (11-ounce) can mandarin oranges,
    drained and chilled
$3/4$ cup Italian salad dressing
2 tablespoons lemon juice
Crumbled bleu cheese to taste

Chop the artichoke hearts. Toss the lettuce, avocado, artichoke hearts, green onions, celery and mandarin oranges together in a large salad bowl. Combine the reserved liquid, salad dressing, lemon juice and bleu cheese in a jar with a tight-fitting lid. Shake well. Pour the dressing over the salad just before serving.

Makes 8 servings

Complementary flavors and textures make this light salad work with almost any meal.

St. Augustine Salad

SALAD
1 cup chopped walnuts
8 ounces mixed greens
8 ounces fresh baby spinach
3/4 cup raisins
8 ounces feta cheese, crumbled

RED WINE VINAIGRETTE
2 tablespoons sugar
4 garlic cloves, minced (optional)
1 tablespoon dried oregano
1/2 cup red wine vinegar
1/2 cup olive oil
1/2 cup chopped red onion (optional)
1/4 teaspoon salt
1/4 teaspoon pepper
1 cup chopped fresh parsley

For the salad, combine the walnuts, greens, spinach, raisins and cheese in a large salad bowl and mix well.

For the dressing, combine the sugar, garlic, oregano, vinegar, olive oil, onion, salt, pepper and parsley in a bowl and mix well. Pour the desired amount of dressing over the salad and toss. Serve immediately.

Makes 8 servings

The crunchy peanut brittle candy topping is just the right twist on this colorful red and green salad.

Strawberry Spinach Salad

SALAD
20 ounces pre-washed fresh spinach
1 quart strawberries, quartered
1 peanut candy bar or 1 piece of peanut brittle, crumbled

CIDER VINAIGRETTE
$1/2$ cup sugar
$1/2$ cup vegetable oil
$1/4$ cup cider vinegar
$1/4$ teaspoon Worcestershire sauce
$1/2$ teaspoon paprika
$1^1/2$ tablespoons minced onion
2 tablespoons poppy seeds

For the salad, combine the spinach, strawberries and peanut candy in a large salad bowl and mix well.

For the dressing, combine the sugar, oil, vinegar, Worcestershire sauce, paprika, onion and poppy seeds in a bowl and mix well. Pour the desired amount of dressing over the salad and toss. Chill, covered, until serving time. Serve the remaining dressing on the side.

Makes 6 to 8 servings

Fresh Tomato Salad

1 tablespoon butter
Kernels of 4 ears fresh white corn
2 pints grape tomatoes, halved
$1/2$ cup (2 ounces) crumbled bleu cheese
1 bunch fresh basil, chopped
1 tablespoon fresh lemon juice
$1/4$ cup olive oil
2 tablespoons balsamic vinegar
$1/2$ teaspoon salt
$1/4$ teaspoon pepper
8 to 10 large Bibb lettuce leaves

Melt the butter in a large saucepan. Add the corn. Sauté over high heat for 3 to
5 minutes. Place the tomatoes in a large bowl. Add the corn, bleu cheese and basil.
Mix the lemon juice, olive oil, vinegar, salt and pepper in a bowl. Pour over the
salad and toss well. Line a large salad plate with Bibb lettuce and mound the tomato
salad on top.

Makes 8 to 10 servings

DÉCOR

*Pretty tables create happy environments. It all starts with the dishes you select. Try to match the
formality of the event with the dishes you choose. A last-minute supper with your neighbors lends itself
to Fiestaware rather than bone china. If you don't have enough place settings of any one pattern, don't
worry—mix and match to create an eclectic look.*

The pomegranate seeds are worth investing in for this tangy, festive salad.

Sweet-and-Spicy Salad

HONEY LIME SALAD DRESSING
Grated zest and juice of 1 lime
1/4 cup mayonnaise
2 tablespoons honey
1 tablespoon vinegar
1 teaspoon chili powder

SALAD
Assorted field greens, radicchio and red leaf lettuce
    equivalent to 1 head of lettuce
1 bunch fresh cilantro, chopped
1/2 to 3/4 cup chopped peanuts
2 to 4 tablespoons pomegranate seeds
1 or 2 apples, cut into bite-size pieces

For the dressing, combine the lime zest, lime juice, mayonnaise, honey, vinegar and
chili powder in a jar with a tight-fitting lid. Cover and shake well.

For the salad, place the greens in a large salad bowl. Pour most of the dressing over
the salad and toss well. Arrange the greens on salad plates. Sprinkle with the cilantro,
peanuts, pomegranate seeds and apples. Sprinkle with the desired amount of dressing.

Makes 4 to 6 servings

Fancy Baked Vidalia Onions

12 small to medium Vidalia onions or other sweet onions
12 slices bacon
Sprigs of fresh rosemary
Salt and pepper to taste
3 tablespoons butter
1 cup sour cream
1 cup (4 ounces) shredded Cheddar, Colby or Swiss cheese
$1^1/2$ cups cheese crackers or butter crackers, crushed
1 egg
Hot sauce to taste

Hollow out the onions, leaving 2 outer layers; reserve the centers. Wrap 1 bacon slice around each onion and secure with a rosemary sprig or wooden pick. Place in a baking dish. Season the onion cavities generously with salt and pepper. Set aside. Finely chop the onion centers. Melt the butter in a skillet. Sauté the onion in the butter. Remove to a bowl and cool for a few minutes. Add the sour cream, cheese, crackers, egg, hot sauce, salt and pepper and mix well. Spoon into the onion cavities. Bake at 300 degrees for $1^1/2$ hours. Cover with foil if the onions begin to get too brown. Increase the oven temperature to 350 degrees during the last 30 minutes if necessary for the filling to set.

Note: If desired, use a combination of cheeses in the filling.

Makes 12 servings

Stuffed Bell Peppers

4 red, yellow or orange bell peppers
2 tablespoons olive oil
3 spicy Italian sausages, casings removed and sausage chopped
1 large sweet onion, chopped
2 portobello mushrooms, chopped
2 (14-ounce) cans chopped tomatoes, drained
5 fresh basil leaves, chopped
1 cup bread crumbs or cooked orzo
$1/2$ cup (2 ounces) grated Parmigiano-Reggiano cheese
Salt and pepper to taste

Bring a large saucepan of water to a boil. Cut the tops off the bell peppers and remove the seeds. Reserve the tops. Place the bell peppers in the boiling water for 4 minutes. Remove and immediately immerse in ice water. Pat dry and place cut side up in a baking dish. Set aside.

Heat the olive oil in a large skillet. Add the sausages. Sauté until partially cooked. Add the onion and mushrooms and cook until the onion is translucent and the mushroom liquid evaporates. Add the tomatoes and basil and cook until heated through. Remove to a mixing bowl. Add the bread crumbs and mix well. Add the cheese, salt and pepper and mix well.

Spoon the sausage mixture into the bell peppers. Cover with the reserved tops. Bake at 350 degrees for 15 minutes. Remove the tops and bake for 15 to 20 minutes longer.

Makes 4 servings

Wasabi Mashed Potatoes

3 pounds russet potatoes
Salt to taste
2 to 3 tablespoons wasabi powder

1 cup milk
$^1/_2$ cup (1 stick) butter, cut into pieces
Pepper to taste

Peel the potatoes and cut into 2-inch pieces. Boil in salted water to cover in a saucepan for 20 minutes or until tender; drain. Mash the potatoes in a bowl. Dissolve the wasabi powder in the milk. Add the milk mixture and butter to the potatoes. Beat until fluffy and smooth. Season with salt, pepper and additional wasabi powder.

Makes 6 servings

A holiday squash specialty that is sure to become a regular family favorite.

Country Club Squash

$^1/_2$ cup boiling water
2 pounds yellow squash, sliced
$^1/_2$ cup chopped onion
1 cup sour cream
$^1/_2$ teaspoon salt
$^1/_4$ teaspoon pepper
$^1/_4$ teaspoon basil

1 cup soft bread crumbs
$^1/_2$ cup (2 ounces) shredded Cheddar
  cheese or Swiss cheese
$^1/_3$ cup butter, melted
$^1/_2$ teaspoon paprika
8 slices bacon, crisp-cooked
  and crumbled

Cook the squash and onion in the water until tender. Drain and mash. Mix the squash mixture and the next 4 ingredients in a bowl. Spoon into a greased 2-quart baking dish. Sprinkle with a mixture of the bread crumbs, cheese, butter and paprika. Top with the bacon. Bake at 300 degrees for 20 to 25 minutes or until heated through.

Makes 8 servings

This tangy side dish contains all of your favorite salad vegetables; hold the lettuce!

Marinated Vegetables

1/4 cup olive oil
1 cup red wine vinegar
2 teaspoons capers
2 tablespoons minced onion
2 tablespoons minced garlic
1 teaspoon hot red pepper flakes

2 teaspoons sugar
1 pound assorted vegetables, such as
    baby carrots, radishes, cucumber
    slices, broccoli florets, cauliflower
    florets and cherry tomatoes

Mix the olive oil, vinegar, capers, onion, garlic, hot red pepper flakes and sugar in a small bowl. Place the vegetables in a large sealable container. Pour the marinade over the vegetables. Seal the container and shake to coat the vegetables. Chill for 3 hours or longer, shaking occasionally. Drain the vegetables and arrange on a serving platter.

Makes 8 servings

These summer vegetables complement any grilled beef, chicken, or fish.

St. Johns Grilled Vegetables

2 yellow squash, cut into 1-inch rounds
2 zucchini, cut into 1-inch rounds
1 red bell pepper, cut into 1/2-inch slices
1 orange bell pepper, cut into
    1/2-inch slices

1/2 Vidalia onion, cut into large chunks
2 teaspoons hot red pepper flakes
1 tablespoon olive oil
Fresh lime juice
Salt and black pepper to taste

Combine the first 5 ingredients in a large bowl. Add the hot red pepper flakes, olive oil, lime juice, salt and black pepper and toss. Place the vegetables in a grilling basket. Grill for 5 to 7 minutes or until the vegetables are browned and slightly soft.

Makes 4 servings

A simple tomato, bacon, and rice dish that looks great served on a bed of romaine lettuce.

San Marco Red Rice

1 cup uncooked rice
2 cups water
4 slices bacon
1 large onion, chopped
1 (14-ounce) can tomatoes
Salt and pepper to taste

Cook the rice in the water in a saucepan using the package directions. Cook the bacon in a skillet until crisp; reserve the drippings. Drain the bacon. Sauté the onion in the bacon drippings in the skillet. Add the tomatoes. Cook until the mixture thickens, chopping the tomatoes as they cook and stirring frequently. Add the cooked rice and mix well. Season with salt and pepper. Spoon into a serving dish. Crumble the bacon over the rice.

Makes 6 to 8 servings

SETTING THE BUFFET

A buffet presentation is the easiest way to serve a large group and offers space to incorporate decorations that reinforce your theme. Serving pieces of varying height save room and add eye appeal. Since guests will be serving themselves, make sure that each dish has the appropriate utensil. Flow is also important. Foods should be arranged logically, in the order in which guests would add them to their plates. Always position toppings, sauces, and dressings immediately following the dish they complement.

Mushroom Risotto

5 cups canned chicken broth
$1/2$ ounce dried porcini mushrooms, rinsed
2 tablespoons butter
1 tablespoon olive oil
$2^1/2$ cups finely chopped onions
12 ounces cremini mushrooms, finely chopped
2 large garlic cloves, minced
1 tablespoon minced fresh thyme
1 tablespoon minced fresh marjoram
$1^1/2$ cups arborio rice
$1/2$ cup dry white wine
$1/2$ cup (2 ounces) grated Parmesan cheese
Salt and pepper to taste

Bring the chicken broth to a simmer in a saucepan. Add the porcini mushrooms. Simmer for 2 minutes or until tender. Remove the porcini mushrooms and finely chop. Set aside. Cover the chicken broth and keep warm over low heat. Combine the butter and olive oil in a saucepan. Add the onions. Sauté over medium heat for 10 minutes. Add the cremini mushrooms and sauté for 8 minutes. Add the porcini mushrooms, garlic, thyme and marjoram. Sauté for 4 minutes. Add the rice and cook for 2 minutes, stirring constantly. Add the wine and cook for 3 minutes or until the liquid is absorbed, stirring frequently. Add 1 cup of the chicken broth. Cook until the liquid is absorbed, stirring constantly. Repeat the process each time chicken broth is added. Cook for 30 minutes or until the rice is tender and the mixture is creamy, stirring constantly. Stir in the cheese and season with salt and pepper. Top with additional cheese if desired.

Makes 8 to 10 servings

Fireworks

Boater's Butter Cake

SAUCE

3/4 cup sugar
1/3 cup butter
3 tablespoons water
1 to 2 tablespoons vanilla extract

CAKE

3 cups cake flour
2 cups sugar
1 teaspoon salt
1 teaspoon baking powder
1/2 teaspoon baking soda
1 cup buttermilk
1 cup (2 sticks) butter, softened
2 teaspoons vanilla extract
1/2 teaspoon almond extract
4 eggs

For the sauce, combine the sugar, butter and water in a saucepan. Bring to a slow boil over medium heat. Remove from the heat. Stir in the vanilla.

For the cake, combine the cake flour, sugar, salt, baking powder and baking soda in a large mixing bowl and mix well. Add the buttermilk, butter, vanilla, almond extract and eggs and mix well by hand. Pour into a greased and floured bundt pan. Bake at 325 degrees for 1 hour to $1^{1}/4$ hours or until the cake tests done. Pierce the hot cake with fork tines. Pour half the sauce over the cake. Cool in the pan for 15 minutes. Remove the cake from the pan. Pour the remaining sauce over the cake.

Makes 8 servings

A classic for chocolate lovers of all ages.

Family Secret Chocolate Cake

CHOCOLATE ICING

$1/2$ cup (1 stick) butter, softened
1 (1-pound) package
   confectioners' sugar

$1/2$ cup baking cocoa
$1/3$ cup water or milk, or to taste
2 tablespoons rum extract

CAKE

2 cups flour
$1^1/4$ teaspoons baking soda
$1/3$ teaspoon baking powder
$1/2$ teaspoon salt
$1^3/4$ cups sugar

$3/4$ cup ($1^1/2$ sticks) butter, softened
3 eggs
$3/4$ cup baking cocoa
$1^1/2$ cups water
1 teaspoon vanilla extract

For the icing, cream the butter in a mixing bowl until light and fluffy. Add the confectioners' sugar gradually, mixing well after each addition. Add the baking cocoa. Add the water 1 tablespoon at a time until the icing is spreading consistency. Stir in the rum extract.

For the cake, sift the flour, baking soda, baking powder and salt together. Cream the sugar and butter in a mixing bowl until smooth. Add the eggs 1 at a time, mixing well after each addition. Add the dry ingredients to the creamed mixture gradually, mixing well after each addition. Combine the baking cocoa and water in a bowl, stirring until the lumps dissolve. Add to the creamed mixture and mix well. Add the vanilla and mix well. Pour the batter into 2 greased and lightly floured 8-inch cake pans. Bake at 350 degrees for 35 to 45 minutes or until a wooden pick inserted in the center comes out clean. Cool in the pans for several minutes. Remove to a wire rack to cool completely. Spread the icing between the layers and over the top and side of the cake.

Makes 12 servings

Chocolate Brownie Torte

BROWNIE CRUST

6 ounces unsweetened chocolate
1 cup (2 sticks) butter
4 eggs, beaten

2 cups sugar
1 tablespoon vanilla extract
$1/2$ cup flour

FILLING

$1/2$ gallon premium vanilla ice cream

3 tablespoons rum

CARAMELIZED BANANAS

4 firm ripe bananas
$1/4$ cup sugar

2 teaspoons fresh lemon juice

SAUCE

$1/2$ cup sugar
$1/4$ cup baking cocoa
$1/2$ cup water

2 ounces semisweet chocolate,
    finely chopped

For the brownie crust, melt the chocolate and butter in a double boiler over simmering water. Stir in the eggs and mix well. Stir in the sugar. Remove from the heat. Stir in the vanilla and flour and mix well. Pour the batter into a 9-inch springform pan. Bake at 300 degrees for 35 to 45 minutes or until a wooden pick inserted in the center comes out clean. Do not overbake. Set aside to cool.

For the filling, place the ice cream in a large bowl to soften. Stir in the rum. Spread the ice cream mixture over the brownie crust and smooth the surface. Wrap tightly and freeze for 12 hours or up to 1 week.

with Caramelized Bananas

For the caramelized bananas, slice the bananas diagonally 1/2 inch thick. Combine the bananas, sugar and lemon juice in a large bowl and toss to coat. Line a large baking sheet with aluminum foil and spray liberally with nonstick baking spray. Arrange the banana slices in a single layer on the baking sheet. Broil 6 inches from the heat source for 3 minutes or until the bananas caramelize. Cool completely.

For the sauce, whisk the sugar, baking cocoa, water and semisweet chocolate in a small saucepan over medium heat for 5 minutes or until smooth. Cover and refrigerate. This can be done up to 1 week in advance. Reheat the sauce before serving.

To assemble, remove the chocolate brownie torte from the pan. Mound the caramelized bananas on top and drizzle with chocolate sauce. Drizzle additional chocolate sauce on the individual serving plates.

Makes 8 to 10 servings

CENTER OF ATTENTION

Look around your home for items that will make interesting centerpieces. A bowl full of vegetables makes a colorful fall arrangement. A scattering of seashells creates a lovely atmosphere, especially when mixed with white votive candles. If you have a fabulous dessert, don't wait to show it off: put it front and center for all to anticipate. Remember—the centerpiece used on a dining table should always be below eye level when guests are seated.

This spicy roll cake tastes great with hot apple cider and a stick of cinnamon.

Three-Spice Pumpkin Roll

FILLING

8 ounces cream cheese, softened
1/2 cup (1 stick) butter or
  margarine, softened

1 teaspoon vanilla extract
1 (1-pound) package
  confectioners' sugar

CAKE

3/4 cup self-rising flour
1 teaspoon ginger
1 teaspoon cinnamon
1 teaspoon nutmeg
3 eggs

1 cup sugar
2/3 cup canned pumpkin
1/2 cup walnuts
1 cup confectioners' sugar
Cinnamon

For the filling, combine the cream cheese, butter, vanilla extract and confectioners' sugar in a mixing bowl and beat until smooth.

For the cake, mix the flour, ginger, 1 teaspoon cinnamon and nutmeg together. Beat the eggs at high speed in a mixing bowl for 5 minutes. Add the sugar and pumpkin and mix well. Add the flour mixture gradually, mixing well after each addition. Spread the batter in a greased and floured 10×15-inch cake pan. Sprinkle with the walnuts. Bake at 375 degrees for 20 minutes. Dust a clean kitchen towel with the confectioners' sugar. Invert the cake onto the towel. Roll the warm cake in the towel from the short end as for a jelly roll and place on a wire rack. Tie the ends of the towel with twist-ties. Chill for 2 hours. Unroll the cake carefully and remove the towel. Spread the filling to within 1/2 inch of the edge of the cake and re-roll. Place seam side down on a serving plate. Cut the roll into slices 1 to 2 inches thick. Serve on plates dusted with cinnamon.

Makes 10 servings

This pound-cake-texture dessert is perfect from picnic to dinner party.

Vanilla Wafer Cake

LEMON GLAZE (OPTIONAL)
1 cup confectioners' sugar
Lemon juice or orange juice

CAKE
$3/4$ cup ($1^1/2$ sticks) margarine, softened
$1^1/2$ cups sugar
6 eggs
3 cups vanilla wafer crumbs (12 ounce package)
$1/2$ cup milk
1 cup chopped pecans
$1^1/3$ cups flaked coconut

For the glaze, place the confectioners' sugar in a bowl. Add enough lemon juice to make a thin glaze.

For the cake, grease and flour a 9-inch tube pan. Line the bottom with waxed paper. Beat the margarine in a mixing bowl until smooth and creamy. Add the sugar and beat until light and fluffy. Add the eggs 1 at a time, mixing well after each addition. Add the cookie crumbs and milk alternately, mixing well after each addition. Stir in the pecans and coconut. (The batter may appear curdled.) Spoon into the prepared pan. Bake at 350 degrees for 1 hour and 10 minutes. Cool in the pan for 10 minutes. Loosen the cake from the side of the pan; remove the waxed paper. Pierce the warm cake with fork tines. Spoon the glaze over the cake.

Makes 10 to 12 servings

Chocolate lovers will swoon over this decadently dark dessert.

Fudge Truffle Cheesecake

FILLING
2 cups (12 ounces) semisweet chocolate chips
24 ounces cream cheese, softened
1 (14-ounce) can sweetened condensed milk
4 eggs
2 teaspoons vanilla extract

CHOCOLATE CRUST
1^{1}/2 cups vanilla wafer crumbs
^{1}/2 cup confectioners' sugar
^{1}/3 cup baking cocoa
^{1}/3 cup melted butter or margarine

For the filling, melt the chocolate chips in a heavy saucepan over very low heat, stirring constantly. Beat the cream cheese in a mixing bowl until light and fluffy. Beat in the milk gradually, mixing until smooth after each addition. Add the melted chocolate, eggs and vanilla and mix well.

For the crust, combine the wafer crumbs, confectioners' sugar and baking cocoa in a bowl and mix well. Stir in the butter. Press onto the bottom of a 9-inch springform pan. Pour the filling into the pan. Bake at 300 degrees for 1 hour and 5 minutes or until the center is set. Cool at room temperature. Chill thoroughly. Refrigerate any leftovers.

Makes 6 to 8 servings

The rich flavors of chocolate and coffee infuse this nontraditional cheesecake.

Mocha Chip Cheesecake

FILLING

24 ounces cream cheese, softened

1 cup sugar

4 eggs, at room temperature

1 tablespoon instant coffee granules

$1/3$ cup heavy cream

1 teaspoon vanilla extract

8 ounces semisweet miniature chocolate chips

CHOCOLATE CRUMB CRUST

$1^3/4$ cups chocolate wafer crumbs (see Note)

3 tablespoons sugar

7 tablespoons unsalted butter, melted

For the filling, beat the cream cheese in a mixing bowl until light and fluffy. Beat in the sugar. Add the eggs 1 at a time, beating well after each addition. Combine the coffee granules and heavy cream in a bowl, stirring until the granules dissolve. Stir the coffee mixture and vanilla into the filling. Beat for 2 minutes.

For the crust, combine the wafer crumbs and sugar in a bowl and mix well. Stir in the butter. Press onto the bottom and halfway up the side of a buttered 10-inch springform pan. Bake at 350 degrees for 10 minutes. Let cool. Pour half the filling into the pan. Fold the chocolate chips into the remaining filling. Pour into the pan. Bake at 200 degrees for 2 hours. Cool at room temperature. Chill, covered, for at least 6 hours.

Note: If you can't find chocolate wafers, use chocolate sandwich cookies with the filling removed. Process to fine crumbs in a food processor or blender.

Makes 12 servings

Molasses Crinkles

$2^1/4$ cups flour
2 teaspoons baking soda
1 teaspoon each cinnamon and ginger
$1/2$ teaspoon ground cloves
$1/4$ teaspoon salt

$3/4$ cup ($1^1/2$ sticks) margarine, softened
1 cup packed light brown sugar
1 egg
$1/4$ cup molasses
1 cup sugar

Mix the flour, baking soda, cinnamon, ginger, cloves and salt together. Cream the margarine and brown sugar in a mixing bowl until light and fluffy. Add the egg and molasses and mix well. Add the flour mixture to the creamed mixture gradually, mixing well after each addition. Chill the dough for 1 hour. Shape the dough by rounded tablespoonfuls into balls. Roll in the sugar. Place 3 inches apart on a greased cookie sheet. Bake at 375 degrees for 10 to 12 minutes. Remove from the cookie sheets immediately. Place on a paper towel or wire rack to cool.

Makes 18 cookies

Extra confectioners' sugar sprinkled on top of these tasty morsels really makes them irresistible.

Rum Confections

2 cups finely crushed vanilla wafers
1 cup finely chopped walnuts
1 cup confectioners' sugar
2 tablespoons baking cocoa

2 tablespoons light corn syrup
$1/3$ cup rum
1 cup confectioners' sugar

Mix the first 6 ingredients in a bowl. Shape by teaspoonfuls into balls. Roll in 1 cup confectioners' sugar. Store in an airtight container. Dust with additional confectioners' sugar before serving.

Makes 24 to 36

Peanut Butter Chocolate Bars

¹/2 cup (1 stick) butter
1 sleeve graham crackers, crushed
1 cup (6 ounces) chocolate chips

1 cup (6 ounces) peanut butter chips
1 (14-ounce) can sweetened
  condensed milk

Melt the butter in a greased 9×13-inch baking pan. Press the graham cracker crumbs over the butter. Layer the chocolate chips and peanut butter chips over the crumbs. Pour the condensed milk over the top. Bake at 325 degrees for 20 to 25 minutes.

Makes 24 to 36

The superb combination of melted chocolates truly makes these the very best brownies.

Southern Brownies

1 cup (2 sticks) butter
4 ounces unsweetened chocolate
2 cups sugar
4 eggs
2 teaspoons vanilla extract
1¹/2 cups flour

1 teaspoon each baking powder and salt
1 cup (6 ounces) white chocolate chips
1 cup heavy cream
2 cups (12 ounces) semisweet
  chocolate chips
1¹/2 cups pecans, toasted and chopped

Melt the butter in a saucepan. Add 4 ounces chocolate. Melt over low heat, stirring constantly. Remove from heat. Stir in the sugar, eggs and vanilla. Add the flour, baking powder and salt. Fold in the white chocolate. Spread in a greased and floured 9×13-inch baking pan. Bake at 350 degrees for 30 minutes or just until the brownies begin to pull away from the sides of the pan. Cool completely. Bring the cream to a boil in a saucepan over low heat. Remove from heat. Add the chocolate chips, stirring until melted. Let stand for 20 to 30 minutes or until the chocolate cools and thickens, stirring occasionally. Spread over the brownies. Press the pecans onto the brownies.

Makes 24

Bride's Pie

GRAHAM CRACKER CRUST
1 to 2 cups graham cracker crumbs (about 18 graham crackers)
1/2 cup sugar
1/2 cup (1 stick) butter, melted

FILLING
2 egg yolks
1 (14-ounce) can sweetened condensed milk
1/2 cup fresh lemon juice
1 teaspoon grated lemon zest
1 tablespoon lemon extract

MERINGUE
2 egg whites
1/2 cup sugar

For the crust, combine the cracker crumbs and sugar in a bowl and mix well. Stir in the butter. Press onto the bottom and side of an 8-inch pie plate. Bake at 350 degrees for 20 minutes.

For the filling, combine the egg yolks and condensed milk in a bowl and mix well. Add the lemon juice, lemon zest and lemon extract, stirring constantly.

For the meringue, beat the egg whites in a mixing bowl until soft peaks form. Add the sugar gradually, beating constantly until stiff peaks form.

To assemble, pour the filling into the crust-lined pie plate. Spread the meringue over the filling, sealing to the edge. Bake at 350 degrees for 15 to 20 minutes or until the meringue is lightly browned.

Makes 6 to 8 servings

The cinnamon and coffee flavors blend smoothly with each bite of silky chocolate almond filling.

Chocolate Almond Silk Pie

PECAN GRAHAM CRACKER CRUST
2 cups graham cracker crumbs
6 tablespoons sugar
$1/4$ teaspoon cinnamon
$1/2$ cup chopped pecans
$2/3$ cup butter, melted

FILLING
2 cups (4 sticks) butter, softened
2 cups confectioners' sugar
4 eggs
4 ounces unsweetened chocolate, melted
2 teaspoons almond, peppermint or hazelnut extract

TOPPING
1 tablespoon instant coffee granules
16 ounces whipped topping

For the crust, mix the cracker crumbs, sugar, cinnamon and pecans in a bowl. Stir in the butter. Press onto the bottom of a 9×13-inch glass baking dish. Bake at 350 degrees for 5 to 8 minutes. Let cool.

For the filling, beat the butter and confectioners' sugar in a mixing bowl. Add the eggs 1 at a time, beating well after each addition. Add the melted chocolate and almond extract, beating until smooth.

For the topping, fold the coffee granules into the whipped topping.

To assemble, pour the filling over the crust. Spread the topping over the filling. Chill until serving time.

Makes 16 servings

A Southern tradition with a twist.

Chocolate Candy Pecan Pie

3 eggs, lightly beaten
1 cup packed brown sugar
1 cup light corn syrup
2 teaspoons butter, melted

1 teaspoon vanilla extract
1^1/4 cups pecan halves or pieces
1 chocolate candy bar, crumbled
1 unbaked (9-inch) deep-dish pie shell

Mix the eggs, brown sugar, corn syrup, butter and vanilla in a bowl. Stir in the pecans and candy bar. Pour into the pie shell. Bake at 350 degrees for 50 to 55 minutes or until a knife inserted near the center comes out clean. Cool on a wire rack.

Makes 8 servings

A great way to have a taste of pecan pie without having a whole slice!

Miniature Pecan Pies

^{1}/2 cup (1 stick) margarine, melted
2 eggs, beaten
1 cup packed light brown sugar
^{1}/2 cup sugar
2 tablespoons milk
1 tablespoon self-rising flour

Pinch of salt
1 teaspoon vanilla extract
1^1/2 cups finely chopped pecans
1 unbaked (9-inch) pie shell
30 frozen miniature phyllo cups, thawed
    and baked

Combine the margarine and eggs in a mixing bowl and mix well. Add the brown sugar, sugar, milk, flour, salt and vanilla and mix well. Stir in the pecans. Pour into the pie shell. Bake at 350 degrees for 45 minutes or until the filling is firm. Cover the pie with a sheet of aluminum foil if it browns too much before the filling is set. Cool the pie. Crumble the pie and crust into the phyllo cups.

Makes 30

A slightly sweet dough accompanies the creamy mascarpone filling with sweet and tart berry flavors.

Tri-Berry Tart

FILLING AND BERRY TOPPING

1/3 cup whipping cream, chilled

1/4 cup sugar

1 cup mascarpone cheese, softened

3 tablespoons orange marmalade

3 tablespoons dark berry liqueur

2 cups each raspberries and blackberries

1 cup blueberries

TART SHELL

1/2 cup (1 stick) cold unsalted butter,
   cut into 1/2-inch cubes

1 1/3 cups flour

2 tablespoons sugar

1/4 teaspoon salt

1 egg yolk

1 1/2 tablespoons ice water

For the filling, beat the whipping cream and sugar until the mixture begins to thicken. Add the cheese and beat until stiff peaks form. Refrigerate mixture if too runny. For the topping, combine the marmalade and liqueur in a saucepan. Simmer until the mixture is reduced to 3 tablespoons, stirring constantly. Let cool slightly. Place the raspberries, blackberries and blueberries in a bowl. Pour the liqueur mixture over the berries and toss gently. The berries may be refrigerated at this point.

For the tart shell and assembly, cut the butter into a mixture of the flour, sugar and salt in a bowl until crumbly. Mix the egg yolk and ice water in a bowl. Add the egg mixture 1 tablespoon at a time to the flour mixture. Stir with a fork until the dough forms a ball. Turn the dough onto a floured surface. Divide into 4 equal portions. Work the dough to distribute the butter. Gather the dough into 1 ball. Flatten into a disk. Chill, wrapped in plastic wrap, for 1 hour and up to 24 hours.

Roll the dough into an 11-inch circle on a lightly floured surface. Fit into a 9-inch tart pan. Pierce the bottom with a fork. Chill for 30 minutes. Line the tart shell with foil and fill with pie weights or dried beans. Bake at 375 degrees for 20 minutes. Remove the weights and foil. Bake for 10 minutes longer or until golden brown. Cool completely. Spoon the filling into the shell. Mound the berries over the filling just before serving.

Makes 8 servings

Mousse au Chocolate

1 envelope unflavored gelatin
1/4 cup cold water
4 ounces unsweetened chocolate, melted
1/2 cup confectioners' sugar
1 cup milk, heated
3/4 cup sugar

1/4 teaspoon salt
1 teaspoon vanilla extract
2 cups whipping cream, whipped
1 cup chopped pecans (optional)
Cookie Cups (below)
Chocolate shavings (optional)

Soften the gelatin in the cold water. Combine the melted chocolate and confectioners' sugar in a saucepan. Stir in the hot milk gradually. Heat just to the boiling point, stirring constantly; do not boil. Remove from heat. Add the gelatin, stirring until dissolved. Stir in the sugar, salt and vanilla. Chill thoroughly. Beat in a large mixing bowl until fluffy. Fold in the whipped cream and pecans. Chill until serving time. Spoon into the Cookie Cups just before serving. Top with chocolate shavings.

Makes 8 servings

Cookie Cups

1/4 cup (1/2 stick) unsalted butter
1/4 cup packed light brown sugar
1/4 cup light corn syrup

3 1/2 tablespoons flour
1/2 cup finely chopped walnuts or pecans
1 teaspoon vanilla extract

Invert a muffin tin on a flat surface. Melt the butter in a saucepan. Add the brown sugar and corn syrup. Bring to a boil, stirring constantly. Remove from the heat. Stir in the flour, walnuts and vanilla. Spoon 3 tablespoons of the batter 6 inches apart onto a greased and floured cookie sheet. Bake at 325 degrees for 10 to 12 minutes. Let cool for 1 minute. Lift each cookie carefully and place over the back of a muffin cup. Press the cookie gently to create a cup. Cool for 3 to 5 minutes. Gently remove the cookie cups to a wire rack to cool completely.

Makes 8

Frozen Tiramisu

1/4 cup freshly brewed espresso or strong coffee
1/4 cup marsala or brandy
1/2 teaspoon vanilla extract
1/2 gallon premium vanilla ice cream
8 toffee candy bars, crushed
2 packages ladyfingers
16 ounces whipped topping
1 cup whipping cream
3 tablespoons sugar
1 tablespoon baking cocoa

Combine the espresso, marsala and vanilla in a small bowl; set aside. Place the ice cream in a large bowl to soften. Stir the toffee crumbs into the ice cream. Add 1/4 cup of the espresso mixture. Line the side and bottom of a 9-inch springform pan with ladyfingers, breaking the ladyfingers to fit if necessary. Spoon the ice cream into the lined pan. Stir 2 tablespoons of the espresso mixture into the whipped topping. Spread over the ice cream. Beat the whipping cream and sugar in a mixing bowl until stiff peaks form. Pipe the sweetened whipped cream onto the top in a decorative fashion. Dust with the baking cocoa. Wrap the springform pan tightly and freeze for 8 hours or up to 2 weeks. Remove the tiramisu 10 minutes before serving.

Makes 12 servings

LIGHTING

Pay special attention to lighting. Dim the overhead lights to flatter your guests, but not so much that they bump into the furniture! Everyone looks better in candlelight, and we all feel better when we look better. Use candles of varying sizes for a romantic atmosphere or use a row of identical large square candles for a contemporary feel. Outdoor lighting is equally important, particularly if the ground is uneven in the party area. Paper lanterns or small white Christmas lights are two fun and attractive ways to light up your night. Always remember, the right lighting will make you and your guests sparkle.

Fresh seasonal berries can also be layered into this already beautiful trifle.

Chocolate Mocha Trifle

1 (18-ounce) package brownie mix
2 (3-ounce) packages white chocolate or
    vanilla pudding and pie filling mix
1³/4 cups cold milk
4 teaspoons instant coffee granules

¹/4 cup warm water
2 cups frozen whipped topping, thawed
3 (1.5-ounce) toffee bars,
    coarsely chopped

Bake the brownies in a 9×13-inch baking pan using the package directions. Cool completely. Whisk the pudding mix and milk in a bowl until the mixture thickens. Dissolve the coffee in the warm water and stir into the pudding. Fold in the whipped topping. Cut the brownies into 1-inch cubes. Layer the brownies, pudding and chopped toffee ¹/3 at a time in a trifle bowl, pressing down slightly on the pudding layers. Chill for 30 minutes before serving.

Makes 12 servings

A light and refreshing dessert for a Florida summer night.

Gin and Tonic Sorbet

²/3 cup sugar
¹/3 cup gin
¹/4 cup fresh lime juice

4 teaspoons grated lime zest
1 (28-ounce) bottle tonic water

Combine the sugar, gin, lime juice and zest in a large pitcher. Stir until the sugar is dissolved. Stir in the tonic water gradually. Chill for 2 hours or up to 3 days. Stir again and pour into an ice cream freezer. Freeze using the manufacturer's directions.

Makes 6 servings

Cranberry Apple Casserole

3 cups chopped peeled apples
2 cups whole cranberries
1/2 cup (1 stick) butter
3/4 cup sugar

1 cup quick-cooking oats
1/3 cup flour
1/2 cup packed brown sugar
1/2 cup chopped pecans

Place the apples and cranberries in a greased 2-quart baking dish. Melt the butter in a saucepan. Remove from the heat. Add the sugar, oats, flour and brown sugar and mix well. Spoon over the fruit. Sprinkle with the pecans. Bake at 350 degrees for 1 hour.

Makes 12 servings

This homey dessert is not only easy and tasty; it makes your kitchen smell divine.

Caramel Baked Apples

8 Jonagold, McIntosh or Gala
  apples, cored
8 large slices lemon peel, 1/4 inch wide
1 cup (or more) packed dark
  brown sugar

2 teaspoons cinnamon
1/4 teaspoon nutmeg
Vanilla ice cream
1 (8-ounce) jar caramel sauce

Place the apples in a 9×11-inch baking dish. Place 1 lemon peel in each apple cavity. Combine the brown sugar, cinnamon and nutmeg in a bowl and mix well. Spoon into the apple cavities, filling to the top. Bake at 400 degrees for 30 to 40 minutes or until the apple peels begin to crack and the apples are tender. Place each apple in a bowl and top with a scoop of ice cream. Drizzle with some of the cooking juices and top with caramel sauce.

Makes 8 servings

The Next Morning

Spicy and hearty, this dish is a meal in itself.

Mayport Shrimp and Grits

GRITS
1 1/2 cups chicken stock
1/2 cup milk
1/2 cup stone-ground or
   quick-cooking grits
1 tablespoon butter

1 to 1 1/2 cups (4 to 6 ounces) shredded
   extra-sharp Vermont white Cheddar
   cheese or Monterey Jack cheese
1 to 2 teaspoons cayenne pepper
Salt and black pepper to taste

SHRIMP
6 to 8 slices bacon, chopped
3 garlic cloves, chopped
1 sweet onion, chopped
5 jalapeño chiles, seeded and
   finely chopped
1/2 cup dry white wine
3 tomatoes, chopped

1 teaspoon paprika
1 to 2 tablespoons Old Bay seasoning
Salt and pepper to taste
1 pound large shrimp, peeled
1/4 cup finely chopped parsley
1/4 cup sliced scallions

For the grits, bring the chicken stock and milk to a boil in a large saucepan. Whisk in the grits. Reduce the heat and simmer for 20 to 30 minutes or until the mixture is thick, stirring frequently. Stir in the butter, cheese, cayenne pepper, salt and black pepper.

For the shrimp, cook the bacon in a large skillet until crisp. Add the garlic, onion and jalapeño chiles. Sauté over medium heat until the onion is golden brown. Add the wine, stirring to loosen any browned bits from the bottom of the skillet. Cook over medium-high heat for 3 to 5 minutes. Reduce the heat to medium-low. Stir in the tomatoes, paprika, Old Bay seasoning, salt and pepper. Add the shrimp. Cook for 5 minutes or until the shrimp turn pink. Remove from the heat. Stir in the parsley and scallions; drain well. Serve over the grits.

Makes 8 servings

Cheesy Sausage Grits

1 pound regular or seasoned bulk pork sausage
Tabasco sauce to taste
$1/3$ garlic clove, minced
$1/2$ teaspoon salt
$1/8$ teaspoon pepper
1 cup quick-cooking grits
2 cups boiling water
2 cups (8 ounces) shredded extra-sharp Cheddar cheese or
    Mexican cheese blend
$1/2$ cup (1 stick) butter, melted
6 eggs, beaten
1 (8-ounce) can chopped mild green chiles (optional)

Brown the sausage in a large skillet, stirring until crumbly; drain. Stir in the Tabasco sauce, garlic, salt and pepper. Cook the grits in 2 cups boiling water using the package directions. Combine the sausage, grits, cheese, butter, eggs and green chiles in a large bowl and mix well. Pour into a generously buttered 9×13-inch baking dish. Bake at 350 degrees for 1 hour. Serve with Cheddar biscuits or corn bread.

Note: Other cheeses can be substituted, or top with a different variety of cheese during the last 5 minutes of baking.

Makes 10 servings

This satisfying pie looks beautiful with a lattice-top crust.

Ricotta Cheese Pie

WHISKEY CRUST

1 1/2 cups flour
1 1/2 teaspoons baking powder
1/2 teaspoon salt
1/2 cup sugar
3 tablespoons butter

1 egg, beaten
1/2 teaspoon vanilla extract or grated
   orange zest
1 tablespoon whiskey or orange juice

FILLING

1 (15-ounce) container ricotta
   cheese, drained
3/4 cup sugar
3 eggs, beaten

1/2 teaspoon vanilla extract
1/2 teaspoon grated lemon zest
1/2 teaspoon flour

ASSEMBLY

1 egg yolk

1 tablespoon water

For the crust, combine the flour, baking powder, salt and sugar in a mixing bowl. Cut in the butter until crumbly. Add the egg, vanilla and whiskey and mix with a fork until the mixture forms a ball. Divide the dough into 2 equal portions and shape each into a ball. Roll 1 ball into a 12-inch circle on a lightly floured surface. Fit into a pie plate.

For the filling, combine the ricotta cheese, sugar, eggs, vanilla, lemon zest and flour in a bowl and mix well.

To assemble, pour the filling into the pastry-lined pie plate. Roll out the second ball of dough and cut into strips. Arrange lattice-fashion over the pie. Beat the egg yolk and water together in a bowl. Brush the egg mixture over the dough. Bake at 350 degrees for 50 minutes.

Makes 8 servings

Dijon mustard is the secret ingredient in this delicious quiche.

Cheese and Asparagus Quiche

1¹/2 pounds fresh asparagus
1 (15-ounce) package refrigerator pie pastry
1 tablespoon butter
1 large Vidalia onion or other sweet onion, chopped
2 tablespoons Dijon mustard
8 ounces Colby Jack cheese, shredded
1¹/2 cups half-and-half
2 large eggs
Salt and pepper to taste

Trim the asparagus to 5-inch lengths. Cook in boiling water to cover for 30 seconds; drain. Immediately plunge the asparagus into ice water to stop the cooking process; drain. Reserve 9 spears. Coarsely chop the remaining asparagus spears; set aside. Unfold the pastries and stack on a lightly floured surface. Roll together into a 14-inch circle. Fit the pastry into an 11-inch tart pan, trimming away any excess dough. Line the pastry with foil. Place pie weights or dried beans in the tart shell. Bake at 425 degrees for 12 minutes. Remove the pie weights and foil. Bake for 2 minutes longer. Cool on a wire rack.

Melt the butter in a skillet over medium-high heat. Add the onion. Sauté for 5 minutes or until tender. Brush the mustard on the bottom and side of the tart shell. Layer with half the cheese, the chopped asparagus, sautéed onion and remaining cheese. Arrange the reserved asparagus spears over the cheese. Whisk the half-and-half, eggs, salt and pepper in a bowl. Pour over the asparagus. Bake at 375 degrees for 25 minutes or until the center is set and the top is golden brown. Let stand for 15 minutes.

Makes 6 to 8 servings

Party Eggs

2 tablespoons Dijon mustard with seeds
12 slices firm white bread
8 slices bacon, crisp-cooked and crumbled
8 ounces diced ham
1 small bunch green onions, chopped
6 ounces Cheddar cheese or Gruyère cheese, shredded
6 ounces Swiss cheese, shredded
9 eggs
3 cups milk
$1/2$ teaspoon salt
$1/4$ teaspoon pepper

Spread the mustard on 1 side of the bread slices. Arrange 6 bread slices mustard side up in a greased 9×13-inch baking dish. Layer half the bacon, ham, green onions, Cheddar cheese and Swiss cheese over the bread. Top with the remaining bread. Whisk the eggs, milk, salt and pepper in a large bowl. Pour over the bread. Layer with the remaining bacon, ham, green onions, Cheddar cheese and Swiss cheese. Chill, covered, for 8 hours. Bake, covered, at 350 degrees for 30 minutes. Bake, uncovered, for 15 minutes longer. Let stand for 10 minutes before serving.

Makes 8 to 10 servings

CHOOSING THE OCCASION

Parties shouldn't wait for the traditional "special occasion." Celebrate joys small and large, or invent your own occasion. A beloved pet's adoption date deserves a blowout as much as any other birthday. Football games, vacations to foreign lands, job promotions, and good report cards are all party-worthy events. What about a weekend when your six favorite friends are in town and available? Is there any better reason?

This dish travels well, as it can be served warm or at room temperature.

Ham and Mushroom Strudel

BÉCHAMEL SAUCE

1/4 cup (1/2 stick) butter
1/4 cup flour
1 cup chicken broth

1 cup milk
Salt and pepper to taste

STRUDEL

2 tablespoons butter
2 green onions, chopped
1 tablespoon chopped shallot
8 ounces mushrooms, sliced
1 1/2 teaspoons herbes de Provence, or
   to taste
1/2 cup chopped honey ham or
   Black Forest ham

Salt and pepper to taste
1 sheet frozen puff pastry, thawed
1/2 cup (2 ounces) shredded
   Gruyère cheese
1 egg
1 to 2 tablespoons warm water

For the sauce, melt the butter in a saucepan over high heat. Sprinkle the flour over the butter. Cook until thickened, stirring constantly. Reduce the heat to medium. Whisk in the chicken broth and milk alternately 1/4 cup at a time, allowing the sauce to thicken before adding more liquid. Season with salt and pepper.

For the strudel, melt the butter in a medium saucepan. Sauté the green onions and shallots in the butter. Add the mushrooms, herbes de Provence and ham. Season with salt and pepper. Cook over low to medium heat until the mushrooms are soft and most of the liquid has evaporated. Set aside. Roll the puff pastry into a 12×18-inch rectangle on a lightly floured surface. Place the puff pastry on a baking sheet. Spread the mushroom mixture down the center of the puff pastry. Spoon 1/4 cup of the Béchamel Sauce over the mushroom mixture and top with the cheese. Fold 1 side over the mixture; fold the other side over the center. Brush the puff pastry with a mixture of the egg and water. Bake at 400 degrees for 30 to 40 minutes or until puffed up and lightly browned. Serve the remaining Béchamel Sauce on the side.

Makes 6 to 8 servings

Egg and Cheese Strata

5 slices buttered bread, torn into small pieces
12 ounces sharp Cheddar cheese, shredded

4 eggs
2 cups milk
Pinch of dry mustard
Crisp-cooked bacon, crumbled

Layer the bread and cheese in a lightly greased baking dish. Lightly beat the eggs in a bowl. Add the milk and mustard and mix well. Pour over the layers in the baking dish. Chill, covered, for 8 hours. Remove the cover. Bake at 350 degrees for 1 hour. Sprinkle with bacon.

Makes 6 to 8 servings

The freshest garden ingredients make this classic scrambled egg dish unique.

Herbed Scrambled Eggs

$1/4$ cup ($1/2$ stick) butter
12 eggs
10 ounces Neufchâtel cheese or light cream cheese, softened
$1/4$ cup chopped scallions
$1/2$ cup chopped fresh basil

$1/4$ cup chopped fresh chives
$1/4$ cup chopped fresh parsley
$1/4$ cup milk
4 teaspoons oregano
1 teaspoon salt
$1/2$ teaspoon pepper

Melt the butter in a large skillet over medium-high heat. Whisk the eggs in a bowl until blended. Add the cheese, scallions, basil, chives, parsley, milk, oregano, salt and pepper. Pour into the skillet. Cook until the eggs are done, stirring constantly to scramble. Serve immediately.

Makes 8 servings

Sunrise French Toast

1 cup packed brown sugar
1/2 cup (1 stick) butter, melted
1 teaspoon cinnamon
3 tart apples, peeled, cored and thinly sliced
1/2 cup dried cranberries or raisins, or both
1 loaf Italian or French bread, cut into 1-inch-thick slices
6 eggs
1 1/2 cups milk
1 tablespoon vanilla extract
2 teaspoons cinnamon
Confectioners' sugar

Combine the brown sugar, butter and 1 teaspoon cinnamon in a 9×13-inch baking dish. Add the apples and cranberries. Toss to coat well. Spread the mixture over the bottom of the dish. Arrange the bread slices on top. Mix the eggs, milk, vanilla and 2 teaspoons cinnamon in a bowl. Pour over the bread. Chill, covered, for 4 to 24 hours. Bake, covered with foil, at 375 degrees for 40 minutes. Uncover and bake for 5 minutes longer. Let stand for 5 minutes. Sprinkle with confectioners' sugar. Serve warm.

Makes 12 servings

FLOWERS

Flowers can set the tone for any celebration. Loose and unconstructed, or neat and formal, the flower, container, and method of arranging communicate your expectations for the event. Be creative when choosing your container; don't limit yourself to vases. Found objects or hollowed seasonal vegetables make festive and inexpensive alternatives. If you are using a glass vase, why not fill it with berries or fruit for added interest.

Warm prior to serving and the cinnamon butter crumb topping will melt in your mouth.

Blueberry Crumb Cake

CRUMB TOPPING

$1/2$ cup sugar

$1/4$ cup flour

$1/2$ teaspoon cinnamon

$1/4$ cup ($1/2$ stick) butter or margarine

CAKE

2 cups sifted flour

2 teaspoons baking powder

$1/2$ teaspoon salt

$1/4$ cup ($1/2$ stick) butter or
    margarine, softened

$3/4$ cup sugar

1 egg, beaten

$1/2$ cup milk

2 cups fresh or thawed frozen blueberries

For the crumb topping, mix together the sugar, flour and cinnamon. Cut in the butter until crumbly.

For the cake, sift together the flour, baking powder and salt. Cream the butter in a mixing bowl. Beat in the sugar gradually. Beat in the egg and milk. Add the flour mixture. Fold in the blueberries. Spread in a greased and floured 8×8- or 9×9-inch cake pan. Sprinkle with the crumb topping. Bake at 375 degrees for 40 to 45 minutes. Cut into squares.

Makes 8 to 10 servings

A light, not-too-sweet recipe that is heavenly with flavored coffee.

Sour Cream Coffee Cake

TOPPING

$1/2$ cup (1 stick) unsalted
   butter, softened
$1/3$ cup plus 1 tablespoon packed light
   brown sugar

$1/4$ cup sugar
1 cup flour
$1/4$ teaspoon cinnamon

CAKE

2 cups flour
1 teaspoon baking powder
$1/4$ teaspoon baking soda
1 teaspoon salt
$1/2$ cup (1 stick) unsalted
   butter, softened

1 cup sugar
2 eggs
1 cup sour cream
1 teaspoon vanilla extract
1 teaspoon almond extract

For the topping, cream the butter, brown sugar and sugar at medium speed in a mixing bowl for 1 minute or until light and fluffy. Add the flour and cinnamon, beating at low speed just until mixed.

For the cake, whisk the flour, baking powder, baking soda and salt together in a small bowl. Beat the butter and sugar at medium speed in a mixing bowl for 3 minutes. Add the eggs 1 at a time, beating after each addition. Add the sour cream and flavorings. Add half the flour mixture, beating at low speed just until combined. Add the remaining flour mixture, beating just until smooth. Pour into a greased 9×13-inch baking pan. Crumble the topping over the cake. Bake at 350 degrees for 35 to 40 minutes.

Makes 10 to 12 servings

Almond Crème Strawberries

2 pints large strawberries, hulled
1 (4-ounce) package vanilla instant
  pudding mix
1 1/2 cups milk
1 1/2 cups whipping cream

1/4 cup sugar
1 teaspoon almond extract, or
  1 tablespoon amaretto liqueur
2 tablespoons confectioners' sugar

Cut a deep X in the stem end of each strawberry. Spread apart to make petals. Prepare the pudding mix using the package directions with 1 1/2 cups milk. Beat the whipping cream and sugar in a mixing bowl until stiff peaks form. Fold into the pudding. Fold in the almond extract. Pipe the pudding mixture into the strawberries using a large writing tip. Arrange in serving dishes. Dust with confectioners' sugar.

Makes 8 to 10 servings

The perfect complement to spiral-cut ham or ice-cold boiled shrimp.

Old-Fashioned Fruit Salad

2 cups red seedless grapes
2 cups green seedless grapes
2 cups drained canned
  mandarin oranges
2 cups fresh or drained canned
  pineapple chunks

2 cups sweetened shredded coconut
2 cups miniature marshmallows
1/2 cup sour cream
1 cup fresh blueberries (optional)
1 cup fresh strawberries, cut into
  halves (optional)

Combine the red grapes, green grapes, mandarin oranges, pineapple chunks, coconut, marshmallows and sour cream in a large bowl. Cover and refrigerate. Refrigerate the blueberries and strawberries separately. Add the berries just before serving.

Makes 20 servings

Chocolate syrup, vanilla ice cream, and coffee make this punch perfect for baby or bridal showers.

Coffee Punch

1 gallon milk
$^1/_2$ cup instant coffee granules
$^1/_3$ cup sugar
1 (16-ounce) can chocolate syrup
$^1/_2$ gallon vanilla ice cream
Whipped cream, cinnamon or chocolate curls (optional)

Heat the milk in a stockpot until just below the boiling point. Combine the milk, coffee, sugar and chocolate syrup in a large container. Chill for 3 hours or longer. Scoop the ice cream into a punch bowl. Pour the milk mixture over the ice cream. Top with whipped cream.

Makes 18 to 24 servings

WHERE AND WHEN

Your guests start to get excited about your celebration from the moment the invitation arrives. Invitations can range from a simple phone call to an elaborate engraved card. Send invitations out in plenty of time so your guests can plan to attend. The standard is two weeks for casual gatherings, three to four weeks for more formal events or during the holiday season.

Thank you for your treasured recipes and your time and talent in testing and tasting every dish.

A Special Toast

We raise our glasses and toast the special members, families, and friends who helped make Toast of the Coast *a celebration of First Coast favorites. So many have helped—please accept our apologies if we inadvertently failed to mention your name.*

Thank you to those listed below for your special contributions and creativity.

Chad Munsey, Proprietor & Sommelier for The Grotto Wine & Tapas Bar, for sharing his "keep it simple" wine philosophy suggestions

Kevin Marshall, Store Manager for Winn-Dixie, who provided generous recipe ingredients for the food photography

Glenn Certain, floral designer, who provided the exquisite flowers used in the photography

Todd and Marlee Krohn, who shared their beautiful porch and oceanfront view for the title page photography

Anita Bahl, Studio Manager for Daryl Bunn Studios, who provided guidance and organization for the cookbook photo shoot

Daryl Bunn, photographer, for his photography expertise, dedication, generous time, and props for the photography

Sherry Warner, food stylist, for her easy and elegant food design

Belk, who sponsored the Mother Daughter Luncheon menu

A special thank-you to our many recipe contributors, who submitted their treasured recipes.

Recipe Contributors

Miriam Strickland Alexander
Nancy Alexander
Denice Anderson
Roxane Andrade
Troy Andrade
Barbara Arnold
Lynn Palmer Bailey
Aleiza Batson
Carrie Bedard
Pam Blumberg
Liz Bobeck
Camille Booth
Edna Bryant
Caroline Busker
Stephanie Cargill
Ashley Carroll
Martha E. Carter
Susan Cheney
Kristen Chmielewski
Virginia Chmielewski
Sean Cokeley
Tara Cole
Emily E. Crawford
Jane Courtney Davis
Susan Dienes
Emily Alexander Dorough
Heather Downey
Kelley Downey
Tracy Duda
Anne Marie Flora

Meg Folds
Lynda Follenweider
Heather Fouts
Karen Freedman
Tricia Freeman
Heather Gardner
Melinda Gibbs
Dawn Gray
Jessamine P. Haff
Joan Haskell
Jill Higginbotham
Kathy Hodge
Cara Hodges
Kelley Hoffman
Hannelore Holland
Suzannah J. Holway
Suzanne Honeycutt
Gayle Houston
Julie Howard
Laura Rose Howell
Judith K. Hughs
Pamela Ilnicki
Alice T. Irving
Anne Jenkins
Genni Jett
Lynne Jones
Mary H. Jordan
Jenny Kage
Kami Lawson
Stacey Lewis
Caroline Lott
Laura Magevney

Paula M. Mathews
Stacey May
Sally McAfee
Bonnie McCormick
Kim McCormick
Sharon McCormick
Kendra McCrary
Catherine McCullough
Peggy McDonald
Cathy McIntyre-Boyd
Julie B. McLaurine
Betsy Miller
Debbie Miller
Michelle Murray Miller
Barbara Mitchell
Jean Mitchell
Mark Mitchell
Dawn Montgomery
Deborah Moore
Susie Morrow
Constance S. Mosseau
Norma Mullen
Paola Parra
Beth Patzke
Nancy Pedrick
Jesse Perry
Connie Phillips
Jody Poulos
Susan Powell
Kathleen Ramsey
Janet Reagor

Jennifer Richards
Andrea Rizzi
Sally F. Robbins
Karlyn Robeson
Jane Anders Ruffin
Bruno Santioni
Christine H. Schmidt
Rebecca Schwam
Ryan Schwartz
Toy Scott
Deborah H. Shaw
Alan Sheppard
Bettina Sheppard
Lara Siewert
Tibby Sinclair
Kimberly C. Skinner
Peter Sledzik
Leigh Hehl Smith
Kim Smithson
Terri Stephens
Sue Stepp
Lisa Ormand Taylor
Millie Taylor
Shayna Thiel
Allison Turknett
David O. Turner
Jill Walker
Laura Wawzynski
Jill Whitaker
Jean Worley
Jenifer Worley

Much appreciation to our recipe testers, who opened their kitchens and helped select recipes.

Kitchen Testers

Roxanne Andrade
Lynn Bailey
Carrie Bedard
Michelle Berrigan
Cindy Berzsenyi
Caroline Busker
Lori Cheanvechai
Kristen Chmielewski
Melissa Coll
Vilma Conmeyer
Jane Covington
Dawn Dorsey
Kelley Downey
Michale Dudley
Katherine Erickson
Kim Farson
Julie Ferguson
Lynda Follenweider
Heather Fouts
Heather Gardner
Jackie Heyl
Christy Hilpert
Suzannah Holway
Jeffrie Hood
Julie Howard

Anne Jenkins
Genni Jett
Lynne Jones
Gina Karr
Laura Kotek
Kami Lawson
Stacey Lewis
Anjali Loeck
Julie Martin
Jennifer Mayo
Bonnie McCormick
Shawn McCormick
Kendra McCrary
Julie McLaurine
Stephanie Minniear
Jean Mitchell
Mark Mitchell
Deborah Moore
Nancy Murrey
Felicia Otterbourg
Paola Parra
Nancy Pedrick
Connie Phillips
Janet Reagor
Jennifer Richards

Karlyn Robeson
Edi Rose
Peggy Rousseau
Heather Sarra
Rebecca Schwam
Jennifer Setzer
Lacy Shaw
Bettina Sheppard
Carrie Sinclair
Kim Smithson
Terri Stephens
Sue Stepp
Shelby Summers
Chassidy Taylor
Shayna Thiel
Jenifer Worley

See page 124 for an index of all recipes.

Menu Index